WJEC
Level 3 Applied Certificate & Diploma
CRIMINOLOGY

STUDY AND REVISION GUIDE

Carole A Henderson
and Laura Neasham

Published in 2019 by Illuminate Publishing Ltd, PO Box 1160, Cheltenham, Gloucestershire GL50 9RW

Orders: Please visit www.illuminatepublishing.com
or email sales@illuminatepublishing.com

British Library Cataloguing-in-Publication Data

A catalogue record for this book is available from the British Library
ISBN 978-1-911208-96-9

Printed by Standartu Spaustuve, Lithuania

02.19

The publisher's policy is to use papers that are natural, renewable and recyclable products made from wood grown in sustainable forests. The logging and manufacturing processes are expected to conform to the environmental regulations of the country of origin.

Every effort has been made to contact copyright holders of material produced in this book. Great care has been taken by the authors and publisher to ensure that either formal permission has been granted for the use of copyright material reproduced, or that copyright material has been used under the provision of fair dealing guidelines in the UK – specifically that it has been used sparingly, solely for the purpose of criticism and review, and has been properly acknowledged. If notified, the publisher will be pleased to rectify any errors or omissions at the earliest opportunity.

WJEC examination questions are reproduced by permission from WJEC.

All web addresses are correct at time of going to press.
Editor: Dawn Booth
Design and layout: Kamae Design
Cover design: Kamae Design
Cover image: domnitsky / Shutterstock

Suggested answers to many of the Activities and Test yourself questions and a few of the Take it further activities and Sample answer questions can be found on the Illuminate website at: http://www.illuminatepublishing.com/WJEC_Crim_SRG_Answers.

Photo acknowledgements

p.1 domnitsky / Shutterstock; p.8 Billion Photos; p.9 Blackboard; p.11 BlueSkyImage; p.13 Lolostock; p.14 MSSA; p.17 bearsky23; p.18 Arpan Rank; p.19 (top) Kathy Hutchins / Shutterstock.com; p.19 (bottom) Twin Design / Shutterstock.com; p.20 (top) Ionndubh; p.20 (bottom) The Clash - I Fought the Law (Official Video); p.21 Lenscap Photography / Shutterstock.com; p.23 Rtimages; p.24 peter dazeley / Alamy Stock Photo; p.26 (right) Photold; p.26 (left) James Boardman / Alamy Stock Photo; p.27 Guennadi Iakoutchik; p.30 Brilliantist Studio; p.31 Steve Parkins / REX / Shutterstock; p.32 Ian_Stewart / Shutterstock.com; p.33 'THINK! Drink Drive: Photocopying #butalive / YouTube; p.35 Barry Barnes / Shutterstock.com; p.36 (top) Courtesy Stop Hate UK; p.36 (bottom) ibreakstock; p.38 Colorlife; p.39 Tero Vesalainen / Shutterstock.com; p.40 Syda Productions; p.42 3dmask; p.43 REDPIXEL.PL; p.44 Lolostock; p.45 Africa Studio; p.47 tynyuk; p.48 Dennis Cox; p.49 Goncharov_Aratem; p.50 Diege Cervo; p.51 Rawpixel.com; p.52 Everett Collection; p.53 (top) Kundra; p.53 (bottom) Lorelyn Medina; p.54 Vladvm; p.56 Alilia Medical Media; p.57 Dirk Ercken; p.58 Public domain; p.59 (top) Andrew Federev; p.59 (bottom) Estilo_Libre; p.64 (top) Max Halberstadt / Public domain; p.64 (middle) INTERFOTO / Alamy Stock Photo; p.64 (bottom) Albert Bandura / Creative commons; p.65 Sybil Eysenck / Creative commons; p.67 Alevtina_Vyacheslav; p.68 Ana Aviskina; p.70 Gwoeii; p.72 (top) VectorsMarket; p.72 (bottom) MicroOne; p.74 (top) Igor Levin; p.74 (bottom) vladimir salman; p.76 MicroOne; p.77 Rawpixel.com; p.78 one photo; p.82 Sinart Creative; p.83 Designua; p.84 chrisdorney; p.85 Mrs_ya; p.86 Rawpixel.com; p.87 (top) sangriana; p.87 (bottom) Olena Yakobchuk; p.89 (top) Arithimedes; p.89 (bottom) smolaw; p.90 (top) petch one; p.90 (bottom) Syda Productions; p.91 TY Lim; p.92 Artist_R; p.93 (top) James Boardman / Alamy Stock Photo; p.93 (bottom) Bobby Turnbull Relative; p.95 Courtesy the Calm Zone; p.96 Steve Maisey / REX / Shutterstock; p.99 Tana888; p.102 alice-photo; p.104 Jemastock; p.105 (top) nienora; p.105 (bottom) Undergroundarts.co.uk; p.106 (top) Audrey_Kuzmin; p.106 (middle) Africa Studios; p.106 (bottom) nevodka p.107 (middle) aerogondo2; p.108 Damaratskaya Alena; p.109 (right) Leonid Andronov; p.109 (left) Alena.Kravchenko; p.110 SpeedKingz; p.111 chrisdorney / Shutterstock.com; p.114 (top) MikeDotta; p.114 (bottom) hafakot; p.115 Jean Faucett; p.117 aquarius83men; p.118 Trevor Christopher / Shutterstock.com; p.120 Sebastian Remme / Alamy Stock Photo; p.122 Aleutie; p.124 Sira Anamwong; p.126 Photo Kozyr; p.127 kenny 1 / Shutterstock.com; p.128 Dan Henson; p.129 (top) James Boardman Archive / Alamy Stock Photo; p.129 (bottom) Allstar Picture Library / Alamy Stock Photo; p.130 dizain; p.131 Richie Chan; p.132 (top) Sudowoodo / Shutterstock.com; p.132 (bottom) SukjaiStock; p.134 alejandro dans neergaard; p.135 maradon 333; p.136 steved_np3; p.137 Courtesy Prison Reform Trust; p.138 Courtesy Sentencing Council; p.140 Alexander Kirch; p.141 r.classen; p.142 hafakot; p.143 Feng Yu; p.144 (right) Teguh Mujiono; p.144 (left) Sabelskaya; p.145 Pkpix; p.146 RAGMA IMAGES; p.147 (top) dizain; p.147 (bottom) felipe caparros; p.148 Why me?; p.149 mindscanner; p.150 GoodStudio; p.151 viktoryabov; p.152 MikeDotta; p.153 bogadeva 1983; p.154 (top) Courtesy of Working Links; p.154 (bottom) Lia Koltyrina; p.155 AVN Photo Lab; p.156 kenny1; p.157 (top) Willy Barton / Shutterstock.com; p.157 (bottom) Naphaphaltharawarin Phen; p.158 (top) Andrey_Popov; p.158 (bottom) Inspiring; p.159 A.P.S. (UK) / Alamy Stock Photo; p.160 Nick Masien / Alamy Stock Photos; p.161 Richard Coombs / Alamy Stock Photo; p.162 (top) Courtesy Prison Reform Trust; p.162 (middle) Courtesy Howard League for Penal Reform; p.162 (bottom) sokolfly; p.165 (top) kristof lauwers; p.165 (bottom left) Creative commons; p.165 (2nd bottom left) Public domain; p.165 (3rd bottom left) Creative commons; p.165 (right) Creative commons; p.166 (top) Tim Large / Alamy Stock Photo; p.166 (bottom); p.168 (top) General Medical Council; p.168 (bottom) Monkey Business Images; p.171 nobeastsofierce; p.172 (top) amasterphotographer; p.172 (bottom) Jemastock; p.173 (top) Nataliya Komarova; p.174 Joseph Sohm / Shutterstock.com; p.175 kenny1; p.176 Photo Veterok; p.177 Willy Barton / Shutterstock.com; p.178 (top) SukjaiStock; p.178 (bottom) Inked Pixels; p.179 (top) Maratyn Williams Photography / Alamy Stock Photo; p.179 (bottom) funnbear63; p.180 (top) Courtesy Prison Reform Trust; p.180 (bottom) Prince's Trust; p.182 FussSeregey; p.185 (top) microstock3D; p.185 (bottom) Harper 3D; p.186 (top) garagestock; p.186 (bottom) Sarawut Aiemsinsuk; p.187 Bakhtiar Zein; p.188 thodonal88; p.189 Wright Studio; p.190 BortN66

CONTENTS

CONTENTS

HOW TO USE THIS BOOK

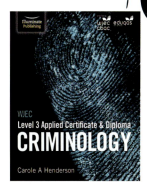

The contents of this *Study and Revision Guide* are designed to support your learning while studying the WJEC Level 3 Applied Certificate or Diploma in Criminology qualification.

This *Study and Revision Guide* will assist in exam preparation and provide ideas for teaching and learning. It has been designed to be used in conjunction with the *WJEC Level 3 Applied Certificate & Diploma Criminology* textbook (ISBN: 978-1-911208-43-3). There are links throughout this guide to the textbook and some of the activities are focused around them. This book supplements the textbook and provides summaries and exam answers to support revision.

The structure of this guide mirrors both the textbook and the course specifications. It is divided into Units and Assessment Criteria (AC). The Certificate in Criminology can be achieved by successful completion of Units 1 and 2. The Diploma requires the additional Units 3 and 4.

Key features

Alongside the revision information in this guide there are key features that will help you to think and prepare you for the controlled assessments or internal assessments, and the external assessments. There are also many activities that may be used within lessons and during personal revision.

Key terms are definitions of key words or terms used within a topic.

Link to textbook shows you where further information can be found and allows you to access this relevant information quickly.

Take it further provides ideas and activities to develop and extend your knowledge.

Controlled assessment tips are suggestions on how to maximise marks in your controlled assessment.

Example questions show you the potential approach of the external exam Units 2 and 4.

Sample answers give examples of answers to show how marks are awarded and how they can be gained/increased.

Exam tips are suggestions on how to maximise marks in an exam.

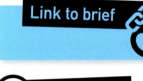

Synoptic links are areas that show how previous parts of the specifications can also apply to other areas. This is particularly important as the exam Units 2 and 4 will contain questions based on other units.

Link to brief, for Units 1 and 3, shows how the learning links to the brief. The brief will be given to you by your teacher.

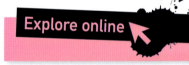

Activities help test your knowledge and reinforce important points for learning. Teachers will be able to utilise some of these in lessons.

Explore online enables you to use the internet to investigate topics and increase your knowledge.

Test yourself provides a series of questions to help you decide if you understand a topic.

Checklists are provided after every AC to allow you to determine if your knowledge is complete.

CHECKLIST – HAVE YOU INCLUDED:

Suggested answers to many of the Activities and Test yourself questions and a few of the Take it further activities and Sample answer questions can be found on the Illuminate website at http://www.illuminatepublishing.com/WJEC_Crim_SRG_Answers.

Skills guidance

There is a section on skills guidance at the end of the guide, which is as important as the information to enable you to achieve. Skills such as evaluation, assessment and analysis are explored with reference to the specifications.

UNIT 1
CHANGING AWARENESS OF CRIME

AC1.1 ANALYSE DIFFERENT TYPES OF CRIME

See pages 14–23 of the textbook.

Analyse each crime by addressing: criminal offences, types of victim, types of offender, level of public awareness and identifying if the crime is deviant and/or criminal.

Controlled assessment tip

Remember this AC is only worth 4 marks, so time management is important! Make sure you include a range of crimes with relevant case examples/case studies.

Types of crime

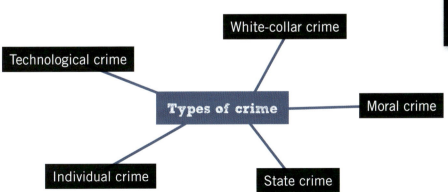

White-collar crime (professional)

The following table is an analysis of white-collar crime.

Criminal offences	Examples include: • computer and internet fraud • credit card fraud • tax evasion • insurance fraud • bankruptcy fraud
Type of victim	People who invest in a financial scheme, such as retired workers and/or those with a substantial amount of money to invest.
Type of offender	White-collar criminals are typically those who work in commercial employment; often people of respectability and high social status.
Level of public awareness	The level of public awareness is low as the crime is often concealed through complex transactions. The public are unaware as sophisticated means and transactions are used in corporate firms and the reputation of the firm is crucial.
Criminal or deviant?	Criminal: actions that are against the law such as fraud. Deviant: actions that break the trust of those who invest with professional financial advisors.
Cases	• Bernie Madoff • Nick Leeson

Key term

White-collar crimes: non-violent crimes traditionally committed in commercial situations for financial gain. White-collar crime is largely committed by a business person wearing a suit and tie.

Activity 1.1

Research the cases of Bernie Madoff and Nick Leeson. Find out:

• what happened in these cases
• how these crimes were concealed from the public.

Controlled assessment tip

You can also cover organised and corporate white-collar crime.

Technological crime may be facilitated by the dark web.

Key term

Technological crimes: committed using a computer and the internet or other electronic technologies.

Explore online

Find online the suggested websites to provide answers to the following:
1. Explain the dark web and the deep web.
2. How can they be accessed?
3. What is Facebook's involvement in the dark web according to the video?
4. Describe the role of the National Cyber Crime Unit.
5. Record brief details of the cyber-attack on TalkTalk in 2015.

Websites:
- NCA (2018) 'What is the Dark Web?' (https://www.youtube.com/watch?v=9nLWbeWWw3E).
- National Cyber Crime Unit (http://www.nationalcrimeagency.gov.uk/about-us/what-we-do/national-cyber-crime-unit).
- BBC News (2015, 6 November) 'TalkTalk Hack "Affected 157,000 Customers"' (https://www.bbc.co.uk/news/business-34743185).

Technological crime

The following table is an analysis of technological crime.

Criminal offences	Examples include: • internet-enabled fraud • downloading illegal matters • hate crime online (cyber-bullying) • downloading copyrighted materials • distribution of malicious code
Type of victim	Anyone who uses the internet. Sometimes, the victim can be a business (as the offender has the intention of gaining access to customer details). However, for specific offences such as cyber-bullying the victim tends to be a young person or vulnerable person.
Type of offender	Typical offenders are those with technical ability. However, for specific offences such as cyber-bullying the offender tends to be a young person.
Level of public awareness	The level of public awareness is low due to the complex nature of technology and often victims are unaware of the crime occurring.
Criminal or deviant?	Criminal: some acts are criminal such as internet-enabled fraud. Deviant: most acts go against norms and values of society.

Individual crime – hate crime

The following table is an analysis of hate crime.

Criminal offences	Examples include: • assault • battery • actual bodily harm (ABH) • criminal damage Remember: hate is an aggravating factor, which is likely to increase the sentence.
Type of victim	Victims could be anyone who falls under the five strands (race, religious belief, sexual orientation, disability or transgender).
Type of offender	Anyone holding prejudicial views against someone falling under the five strands. Typically, those with traditional views.
Level of public awareness	Public awareness has grown recently due to increased media attention; however, some still do not know acts that constitute hate crime.
Criminal or deviant?	Criminal: the acts are criminal in nature (assault, ABH, etc.). Deviant: actions are regarded as deviant as the views are prejudicial based on identity.
Cases	• Matthew Shepard • Adam Pearson

Key term

Hate crimes: targeted at a person because of hostility or prejudice towards the person's disability, race or ethnicity, religion or belief, sexual orientation or transgender identity.

Activity 1.2

Research the following cases, recording the facts of the hate crimes that occurred:

• Matthew Shepard
• Adam Pearson.

Explore online

Watch the following YouTube video to answer the questions below:
• 'What is Hate Crime?' (https://www.youtube.com/watch?v=kkgVZ5CzyqA).
1. Give a definition of hate crime.
2. What are the strands of hate crimes?
3. Give four examples of hate crimes.
4. How can hate crimes be reported?

Individual crime – domestic abuse

The following table is an analysis of domestic abuse.

Criminal offences	Examples include: • assault • murder • ABH/grievous bodily harm (GBH) • rape
Type of victim	Typically, female victims in an intimate relationship.
Type of offender	Typically, males in an intimate relationship.
Level of public awareness	Public awareness can be regarded as low as it is a domestic crime that is often hidden by the victims. However, society is very much aware it occurs, yet do not know the true extent.
Criminal or deviant?	Criminal: the acts are criminal (assault, murder, etc.). Deviant: actions are regarded as deviant as it is regarded as abusing power in a relationship of trust.
Examples	• Casey Brittle • Tina Nash

Key term

Domestic abuse: an incident or pattern of incidents of controlling, coercive, threatening, degrading and violent behaviour, including sexual violence, in the majority of cases by a partner or ex-partner, but could also be by a family member or carer.

Activity 1.3

Research the following cases:
• Casey Brittle
• Tina Nash.

Write a short paragraph using these cases to explain the impact of the police failing to intervene in domestic abuse cases.

Take it further

Domestic abuse: research the case of Alex Skeel and consider how it challenges the concept about victims of domestic abuse typically being female.

CHECKLIST – HAVE YOU INCLUDED:

- [ ] a range of crimes – four needed for 4 marks
- [ ] clear analysis, including: criminal offences, typical victim, typical offender, level of public awareness, and deviant and/or criminal
- [ ] examples (case studies)
- [ ] links to the assignment brief?

Controlled assessment tip

Do not forget to make reference to the assignment brief for all relevant crimes.

AC1.2 EXPLAIN THE REASONS THAT CERTAIN CRIMES ARE UNREPORTED

See pages 24–28 of the textbook.

Controlled assessment tip

Remember this AC is only worth 4 marks, so time management is important. Make sure you include reasons why a range of crimes may go unreported, using relevant examples throughout. In this instance, the use of 'examples' refers to the various crimes/offences that go unreported. Remember, the assignment brief could always be used as a relevant example.

Make sure you consider the reasons and crimes listed in the specification.

Activity 1.4

Reasons for not reporting crimes

Place the crimes shown at the top of the following page next to the relevant reason for not reporting them in the table below. Some may have more than one reason.

Personal reasons		Social and cultural reasons	
Fear		Lack of knowledge	
Shame		Complexity	
Disinterest		Lack of media interest	
Not affected		Lack of current public concern	
		Culture-bound crime	

Crimes:

Common assault	Criminal damage	Hate crime
Domestic abuse	Littering	Under-age drinking
Honour crime	Petty theft	Illegally downloading
Vandalism	White-collar crime	music
Rape	Vagrancy	Cyber-bullying
Sexual offences	Assisted suicide	Prostitution

Personal reasons

Fear

Some choose not to report crimes out of fear of the consequences. When domestic abuse or honour crime occurs, often the victims are scared of the offender and this fear prevents them reporting the crime to the police. Some victims may also fear for their family or may also fear not being believed – this is often the case with rape or sexual offences.

Shame

If a crime involves a sexual act (rape), this can often prevent someone reporting the crime. Those involved may be embarrassed or ashamed due to the perception of vulnerability in such offences.

Not affected

Often, when crimes occur, those who are not involved do not feel compelled or motivated to report it. Some take the view that it is simply 'none of my business'. This is often the case for crimes such as vandalism and/or criminal damage if it is not their property. Likewise, moral crimes such as vagrancy and under-age drinking are not reported, as people perceive such crimes as victimless, hence not affecting anyone. Petty theft and littering are also relevant examples here.

Social and cultural reasons

Complexity

When crimes are particularly complex the public may find it challenging to acknowledge such offences, for example many people have a limited understanding of white-collar crime due to the complexity of fraudulent transactions, which are also largely concealed by companies. Complex crimes are very difficult to trace, making it difficult to report them.

Fear is a reason why victims fail to report domestic crime.

Lack of media interest

Often, moral crimes or low-level crimes are not widely promoted by the media as they normally attract little public interest. Certain crimes are not considered a social problem and therefore feature rarely in the media. Some people then choose not to report these crimes as they may not be aware of the true extent of them (how often the crimes actually occur). This is particularly true for under-age drinking, prostitution, littering, petty theft and common assault.

Culture-bound crime

Some culture-bound crimes may be regarded as acceptable by some individuals, based on cultural beliefs and/or tradition, for example honour killings and female genital mutilation. Those not involved may fail to report such offences due to the lack of knowledge and understanding of such cultural beliefs, making it difficult to acknowledge a crime like this in the first place. Others may feel that cultural diversity is mystifying and simply choose to ignore such crimes in order to avoid interfering.

LIVE REPORT

Some crimes are unreported due to the lack of media interest.

Key term

Culture-bound crime: tends to belong to a particular culture. Examples include honour killing, witchcraft and female genital mutilation.

Controlled assessment tip

Do not forget to make reference to the assignment brief to explain the reasons why crimes may be unreported.

Explore online

Why is rape an unreported crime?

Access 'The Criminal Justice System: Statistics' on the RAINN website below and answer the questions that follow:
· 'The Vast Majority of Perpetrators Will Not Go to Jail or Prison' (https://www.rainn.org/statistics/criminal-justice-system).
1. Out of every 1,000 rapes, how many are reported to the police?
2. How many female students will report rape?
3. What are the three most common reasons for not reporting rape?
4. What are the three most common reasons for reporting rape?

CHECKLIST – HAVE YOU INCLUDED:

- [ ] personal and social/cultural reasons (a range)
- [ ] a clear and detailed explanation of the reasons
- [ ] examples (crimes/offences)
- [ ] links to the assignment brief?

AC1.3 EXPLAIN THE CONSEQUENCES OF UNREPORTED CRIME

See pages 29–33 of the textbook.

Sample answer

Read the response to AC1.3 and the annotations below.

There are a number of consequences of unreported crime, including: a ripple effect, decriminalisation, police prioritisation, unrecorded crime, cultural change and legal change.

The ripple effect describes how the effects of a crime can spread beyond the victim. It may affect others such as family, friends or even the community. For example, if a burglary were to occur in a residential street, the negative consequences would impact the homeowner, as they may fear returning home. However, this could cause a ripple effect as it may also affect other homeowners in the street. The area may attract a negative reputation and house prices may decrease. Domestic abuse can also create a ripple effect as often abusers may come from an unstable environment where they have experienced/witnessed abuse. This illustrates how, if crimes go unreported, the negative effects may impact those surrounding the victim.

Decriminalisation occurs after laws have been frequently altered as they cannot be imposed or enforced. Often, crime is not reported due to a lack of public concern or interest, this means that, over time, the government has little choice but to decriminalise the act. Essentially, there are still laws against it, however the punishments have changed – or in some cases it may even be legalised. An example of this is homosexuality. This can be a positive consequence for society.

Police prioritisation is used so that the police can focus their time on the most pressing matters in that area. For instance, Durham Police have different attitudes towards cannabis from elsewhere in the UK, where they believe low-level cases should result in support and rehabilitation, as opposed to prosecution. This is so that the more important crimes are given more attention.

Controlled assessment tip

To achieve top marks, make sure you can identify if a consequence of unreported crime has a positive or negative effect on the individual/society.

Ripple effect clearly described with a relevant example.

Decriminalisation accurately explained and a correct example given. Candidate is aware of the difference between decriminalisation and legalisation.

Police prioritisation explained clearly.

Candidate could outline whether police prioritisation is a positive or negative consequence, to improve the response.

When crimes are reported to the police, they are not always recorded by them. This is sometimes purposely done to make it look like the crime rates are decreasing, or caused by workload pressures and inadequate supervision. In 2014, the police failed to record one in five of all crimes reported to them, and the problem is greater for more violent offences. Due to this, the public may lose faith in the police and may choose not to report crime again in the future. This may also encourage offenders to commit more crime as they could believe that they are getting away with it.

Cultural change may be considered a negative consequence for the community. The broken windows theory suggests that unchecked and unreported minor crimes lead to further and more serious crimes. An uncared-for area can act as a magnet for delinquent behaviour. For example, if an area becomes run-down and properties are vandalised, poverty can push people into prostitution, drug use and other petty crimes. More crimes are then committed as no one reports more serious crimes such as rape or murder. The idea is that poverty breeds poverty, and poverty breeds crime – if a street looks particularly rough or is known for crime, it is unlikely that anyone would want to buy a house there. When the whole area becomes labelled as a magnet for crime, there is no source of income for the local area and this makes people turn to crime. If all crime was tackled in the first place, crime rates in the area would likely decrease.

Legal change can be a positive consequence of unreported crime. Homosexuality was illegal in the UK until 1967, but due to social changes and a lack of stigma the law changed. People were no longer reporting homosexuality, as society no longer agreed with the law. The law was changed so that it is no longer illegal. Gay marriage is now legal and more than 15,000 marriages have taken place since it was legalised.

Example used to illustrate the consequence.

Very clear explanation of unrecorded crime with statistic to support explanation.

Negative consequence outlined as candidate is stressing that crime would continue to occur.

Negative consequence outlined.

Clear and detailed explanation.

Candidate identifies that legal change can be regarded a positive consequence.

Homosexuality used as an example.

Statistics to support the consequence.

Well written, good use of specialist terminology used throughout.

Six consequences of unreported crime explained clearly and in sufficient detail. The response includes relevant examples and statistics to support the explanation.

Activity 1.5

Refer to the mark band criteria below for AC1.3 and mark the sample response shown on pages 15–16. How many marks would you award it out of 4?

pages 15–16

Controlled assessment tip

Remember, there are only 4 marks available here, so consider time management. It is advised to try and cover as many consequences as possible but briefly.

ASSESSMENT CRITERION	MARK BAND 1	MARK BAND 2
AC1.3 Explain the consequences of unreported crime	Limited explanation (may only list examples) of the consequences of unreported crime **(1–2)**	Clear and detailed explanation (includes relevant examples) of the consequences of unreported crime **(3–4)**

Link to brief

Mr and Mrs S Brief

A consequence that may occur in the brief should the crimes not be reported is a ripple effect. Mr S is abusing his wife, Mrs S, this is clearly domestic abuse. Should the son and daughter witness this, it may cause a ripple effect in the future by leading to further abuse, for example the children may then commit violent offences in the future, based on what was witnessed as a child. In addition, Mrs S' family, friends and work colleagues may be affected should Mrs S confide in them or if she is absent from work.

CHECKLIST – HAVE YOU INCLUDED:

- [ ] a clear and detailed explanation of the consequences of unreported crime (a range)
- [ ] examples
- [ ] link(s) to the assignment brief?

Time management is important. It is an eight-hour assessment.

AC1.4 DESCRIBE MEDIA REPRESENTATION OF CRIME

The specification lists the following media forms: newspaper, television, film, electronic gaming, social media (blogs, social networking) and music. Try to include all of these media forms when describing how the media represents crime.

See pages 34–37 of the textbook.

Activity 1.6

Match the important term to the definition in the table below.

Important term	Definition
	To cause events (especially in newspaper reports) to seem more vivid, shocking, etc. than they really are.
	To say something has happened more times than it has.
	Tending to intrude on a person's thoughts or privacy.
	To make something seem better than it is and therefore more attractive.
	To describe falsely an idea, opinion or situation.
	Describe or represent as admirable, especially unjustifiably.
	To spread stories that cause public fear.
	To add or change some details of a story, usually to make it more interesting or exciting.

Important terms: sensationalise, glamorise, over-report, invasive, scaremonger, misrepresent, glorify, embellish

Controlled assessment tip

This AC is 6 marks, thinking about time management you should allocate a little more time than the three previous ACs when in the controlled assessment.

Controlled assessment tip

The command word for this AC is DESCRIBE. You do not need to evaluate or assess the impact of the media representation, just describe it.

Television plays a major role in the portrayal of crime by the media.

Controlled assessment tip

Try to use these terms when describing the media representation of crime. For example, some films tend to *glamorise* crime, for example the film *The Wolf of Wall Street* makes white-collar crime and drug use appear *glamorous* by linking such crimes to material possessions.

Key points

By and large, the media tend to sensationalise crime, whether this be through fictional or factual representations.

- **Newspapers** devote a vast amount of coverage to crime, including terrorist attacks, rape, murder and gang crime. Using imagery and dramatic headlines, newspapers grip the reader, as crimes, or the rate of crime, are often exaggerated or misrepresented.

- **Television** is also saturated with crime. Fictional TV shows such as *Law and Order*, *Midsomer Murders* and *Broadchurch* all use powerful and emotional imagery or storylines to attract viewers. Police are largely portrayed as successful, arresting criminals or seeking justice. Criminals are largely portrayed as 'evil' with sensationalised crimes.

- Factual programmes such as *Crimewatch* and *24 Hours in Police Custody* portray a wider range of crimes and often represent real police procedure, not simply thrilling investigative techniques such as those often heavily represented in fictional shows, while letting the audience become more acquainted with the criminal and their experiences.

- **Film** glamorises crime. Films such as *The Wolf of Wall Street* (right) make white-collar crime and drug use appear glamorous by linking such crimes to material possessions and lifestyle. Films such as *The Godfather* and *American Gangster* portray gang crime and drug lords in a sensationalised way, with dramatic scenes featuring violence, money or intense police chases. Many films are focused solely around crime and such films are often classified as requiring an accompanying adult for those under the age of 15 years, due to the severity of crime involved.

- Crime is now also heavily featured in **electronic gaming**. Games such as *Grand Theft Auto*, *Mafia* and *Payday* all feature crime. *Grand Theft Auto*, despite being an age 18 title, is often played by those much younger, at time of writing, and has total sales of 90 million copies worldwide. *Grand Theft Auto* can trivialise crime, suggesting that crime and violence are acceptable, often appearing exciting or thrilling as players are required to commit crimes to achieve game points.

- **Social media** is now used to report crimes. Police forces use Facebook and Twitter to keep the public up-to-date with crime in particular geographical locations. Facebook also enables people to 'check in' to allow their followers to know they are safe during tragic incidents such as terrorist attacks, highlighting how terror attacks and crimes can be portrayed to the public. Social media is also now widely used to share photos or videos of incidents involving crime, taken by members of the public. Some of these photos or videos can be distressing or portray violence.

Police forces now use Twitter to share news.

- **Music** also features crime. For years, songs such as 'I Fought the Law' and 'Bonnie and Clyde' have featured crime. However, more modern artists such as Eminem and Tupac have also made songs referencing gangs, crime, sex and drugs, again sensationalising crime.

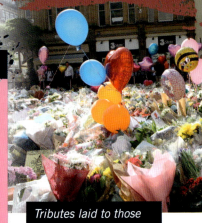

Explore online

To access mark band 2 and achieve 4–6 marks in this AC, relevant examples are needed. Use the articles on the websites below, as well as the video links, to research examples of the media representation of crime. This should help ensure that your description is detailed.

For each example, answer these two key questions:
1. What type(s) of crime is/are portrayed?
2. How does the media describe the crime(s)?

Newspapers:
- Emily Banks (2018, 8 June) 'Moped Gangs Have a Terrifying New Tactic …', *Daily Mail* (http://www.dailymail.co.uk/news/article-5822785/Moped-muggers-new-tactic-Gangs-target-parents-school-run.html).
- Mark Hodge (2017, 24 May) '"Attack on Innocence", Manchester Attack …', the *Sun* ('https://www.thesun.co.uk/news/3636785/manchester-attack-newspapers-around-world-reaction-pictures-suicide-bombing/).

Television:
- 'Crimewatch UK – June 2014' (https://www.youtube.com/watch?v=RWuydw2fdTU).
- 'Acorn TV / Midsomer Murders / Series 17 Clip' (https://www.youtube.com/watch?v=79Rn27krUxM).
- 'Broadchurch Official Trailer HD' (https://www.youtube.com/watch?v=HOnus6OvViM&t=9s).

Film:
- 'Jack Reacher Official Trailer #1 (2012) - Tom Cruise Movie HD' (https://www.youtube.com/watch?v=A7FiWkyevqY).

Electronic gaming:
- 'Grand Theft Auto V: The Official Trailer' (https://www.youtube.com/watch?v=hvoD7ehZPcM).

Social media:
- 'Metropolitan Police' (https://twitter.com/metpoliceuk?ref_src=twsrc%5Egoogle%7Ctwcamp%5Eserp%7Ctwgr%5Eauthor).

Music:
- 'The Clash – I Fought the Law (Official Video)' (https://www.youtube.com/watch?v=AL8chWFuM-s).

Tributes laid to those who died in the Manchester attack.

A screenshot from The Clash's video for 'I Fought the Law'.

CHECKLIST – HAVE YOU INCLUDED:

- [ ] all media forms, including: newspaper, television, film, electronic gaming, social media and music
- [ ] a detailed description of the media representation of crime, covering both fictional and factual representation
- [ ] relevant examples (TV shows, films, etc.)?

AC1.5 EXPLAIN THE IMPACT OF MEDIA REPRESENTATIONS ON THE PUBLIC PERCEPTION OF CRIME

See pages 38–42 of the textbook.

Activity 1.7

Consider the newspaper headlines in the image below.
1. What impact could these headlines have on the public?
2. How influential are media representations when it comes to the public perception of crime?

The impact of media representations on the public perception of crime

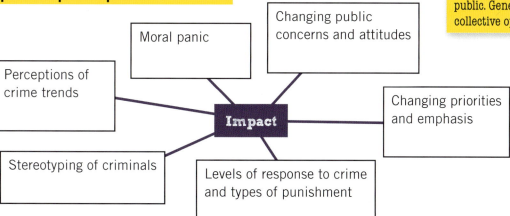

Controlled assessment tip

This AC should not be a repetition of AC1.4. When addressing AC1.5 in the controlled assessment make sure you explain the impact of the media representations of crime. You must explicitly address how the media portrayal of crime impacts public perception.

Key terms

Impact: the effect or consequence of something. In this instance, what effect the media representation of crime has on the public.

Public perception: the perceived level of crime in a particular place, or the perceived severity of crimes. It is the opinion or belief held by the public. Generally, it is a collective opinion.

Activity 1.8

1. Add key explanations for each impact onto the mind map on the previous page.
2. Add specific examples of media portrayals when explaining the impacts on your diagram.
   - Example: The media portrayal of the Mods and Rockers was an example of a moral panic. *Place it under the Moral panic impact.*
3. Add the following examples to your diagram:
   - Terror attacks (including Manchester, London and Barcelona)
   - Islamophobia
   - Anti-terrorism Crime and Security Act 2001, Counter-Terrorism Act 2008, airport security, prevent strategy, youth crime
   - Hoodies
   - London riots
   - Crime Survey of England and Wales (statistics about the rate of crime)
   - Knife crime
   - HIV

If you need some hints to help you complete this activity, see pages 38–42 of the textbook and summarise the full explanation for each impact.

CHECKLIST – HAVE YOU INCLUDED:

- [ ] a clear and detailed explanation of the impact of a range of media representations on the public perception of crime
- [ ] explicit reference to the public perception of crime
- [ ] specific examples?

Explore online

Stereotyping of criminals

Read the article mentioned below, then answer the following questions:

- Dr Carolyn Côté-Lussier (2016, 8 February) 'Debunking Stereotypes of Criminals' (https://www.lawgazette.co.uk/commentary-and-opinion/debunking-stereotypes-of-criminals/5053490.article).

1. How are criminals in the UK stereotyped?
2. How does this stereotyping affect the public?
3. Why would the public support harsh sentences as a result of stereotyping?
4. How has this affected the prison population?
5. What suggestions does the article put forward to challenge this?

AC1.6 EVALUATE METHODS OF COLLECTING STATISTICS ABOUT CRIME

See pages 43–47 of the textbook.

Activity 1.9

Answer the following three questions:
1. How are statistics about crime collected in England and Wales?
2. Which professionals/professional bodies would collect statistics about crime?
3. What is the purpose of collecting crime statistics?

Controlled assessment tip

This AC requires EVALUATION for 6 marks. Keep the description of the methods very brief and make sure the evaluation is detailed.

Methods

- Home Office statistics: use police-recorded crime. Every offence recorded by the police will feature in the statistics.
- Crime Survey for England and Wales: uses a survey, in the form of a questionnaire sent to households.

Remember, use the key evaluation criteria listed by the specification: reliability, validity, ethics of research, strengths and limitations, and purpose of research.

Make sure this AC is written in clear paragraphs, it needs to be detailed in order to gain 6 marks.

Controlled assessment tip

For the controlled assessment, you need to evaluate two sources of information only: Home Office statistics (police-recorded crime – PRC) and the Crime Survey for England and Wales. You should evaluate the *methods* used to collect these statistics.

For a definition of each evaluation criterion, refer to page 45 of the textbook.

The Crime Survey for England and Wales is a victim survey posted to households.

Evaluation of methods

Home Office statistics: the strengths and limitations of police-recorded crime statistics.

Strengths	Limitations
• Police can record crimes accurately as the data will be based on reports and arrests. • Police can communicate with offenders and victims regularly to ensure valid data is recorded (the data is accurate). • The police can investigate crimes further to make sure all incidents are recorded. • Police can monitor crimes based on geographical area and time period to help detect crimes or prevent further crime. • Police can use the statistics of recorded crime to inform new initiatives and policies. • Police can compare crime statistics on an annual basis to generate trends and patterns.	• Police do not record all crime reported to them. • Police-recorded crime does not contain details of unreported crime. This is often referred to as the dark figure of crime. • Police forces may use a variety of recording practices, which may produce unreliable data (lack of standardised procedure across forces). • Variation in recording practices also reduces the effectiveness of annual comparisons. For example, crime trends may appear to be decreasing when it is merely a change in procedure (this may lack validity). • Some victims may be reluctant to communicate with police officers due to fear, embarrassment, etc.

The Crime Survey for England and Wales (CSEW): the strengths and limitations.

Strengths	Limitations
• CSEW captures unreported crime, as victims may feel more confident to report one when completing a survey because the results remain anonymous (relevant for victims who do not report due to fear or embarrassment).	• CSEW fails to capture victimless crimes. • CSEW fails to capture crimes that are very difficult to detect such as white-collar crime.

(Continued)

Strengths	Limitations
• CSEW relies on first-hand knowledge from the victim, which may increase validity as it is not interpreted by a police officer. • CSEW identifies those who are most likely at risk to be potential victims, which can inform crime prevention strategies. • CSEW covers a large sample. • CSEW may provide rich, qualitative data that is valid, as the victim may feel less pressure to provide details because there is no risk of identification. • CSEW is confidential and participants do have the right to privacy. Participants can refuse to complete the survey, which ensures that ethical guidelines are followed. • CSEW achieves informed consent that the participant is willingly completing the survey. • CSEW is regarded as more reliable than police-recorded data.	• CSEW may fail to capture crimes such as domestic abuse because participants may refuse to complete the survey due to fear in their own household. • Participants may lie or exaggerate on the CSEW, making the data invalid. • CSEW relies on the accuracy of the victim's memory. • The sample may not be representative of the general population. Participants who are most likely to complete such surveys may include the elderly, unemployed or students, due to fewer time limitations. • The sample is large; however, the survey is not sent to every member of the public. • Victims may be reluctant to complete the CSEW for fear it may not be confidential. • The results require interpretation: may include bias, which negatively affects validity.

Key point

There is a lack of parity between the two methods of collecting crime statistics. The Home Office Statistics reported a 10% rise in crime in 2017, whereas the CSEW reported a reduction of 7%. This indicates that both sources of information have limitations.

Refer to pages 46–47 of the textbook to consider a sample answer that achieved 5 marks. Improve this answer using the above table to ensure it can achieve 6/6.

CHECKLIST – HAVE YOU INCLUDED:

- [ ] the two sources of information about crime: Home Office statistics (PRC) and the Crime Survey for England and Wales
- [ ] a clear and detailed evaluation of the methods used to collect crime statistics – both information sources require evaluation
- [ ] evaluation criteria: reliability, validity, ethics of research, strengths and limitations, and purpose of research?

LEARNING OUTCOME 2 UNDERSTAND HOW CAMPAIGNS ARE USED TO ELICIT CHANGE

AC2.1 COMPARE CAMPAIGNS FOR CHANGE

See pages 48–54 of the textbook.

Activity 1.10

Use pages 49–51 of the textbook to help you complete the comparison table below for the two campaigns for change.

Campaign for change: Sarah's law		Campaign for change: Brexit	
Purpose of the campaign (to change policy, raise awareness, etc.)		Purpose of the campaign (to change policy, raise awareness, etc.)	
Focus (criminal law, constitutional law or other)		Focus (criminal law, constitutional law or other)	
Driving forces behind the campaign (individuals/ organisations, etc.)		Driving forces behind the campaign (individuals/ organisations, etc.)	
National or local campaign		National or local campaign	
Campaign methods/ media		Campaign methods/ media	
Celebrity support		Celebrity support	
Success (was the campaign successful, partially successful? What changes did it bring?)		Success (was the campaign successful, partially successful? What changes did it bring?)	

Campaigns for change

Some campaigns for change are listed below; however, this list is not exhaustive. You can select any campaign for change to include in AC2.1. The campaigns for change do not have to relate to a crime, in fact it is advised to have a range of campaigns to allow you to make more detailed comparisons:

- Sarah's law (Child Sex Offender Disclosure Scheme)
- Clare's law (Domestic Violence Disclosure Scheme)
- Helen's law
- Lillian's law
- Ann Ming: double jeopardy
- anti-smoking campaigns
- Brexit
- LGBT campaigns
- Scottish independence
- abortion campaigns
- anti-fox hunting.

Anti-smoking campaigns could be used when drawing comparisons in this AC.

How to structure this AC in the controlled assessment

This AC should be written in paragraphs in the controlled assessment. To achieve 8–10 marks your comparison needs to be 'clear and detailed'. Avoid lengthy descriptions about each campaign, focus on the comparisons.

You may wish to structure this AC as follows but remember that this is only a suggestion:

- You could have paragraphs on the various comparisons (e.g. purpose and driving forces, etc.) rather than a paragraph on each campaign. Warning: a paragraph on each campaign tends to become descriptive and lacks detailed comparisons, resulting in low marks.
- Within the paragraphs you should include a range of campaigns for change, not just two campaigns.

Paragraphs to use

- **PURPOSE**: what purpose do the campaigns have? To change law and policy, attitudes or funding? You could also consider the focus of the campaign – criminal law, constitutional law, etc.

Controlled assessment tip

This AC requires a comparison, you should focus on similarities and differences between a range of relevant campaigns for change. You may find it useful to create a table, similar to the one above, for all of your chosen campaigns *before* starting to write a detailed comparison in the controlled assessment. A minimum of five campaigns should be studied; however, the more campaigns you include, the more opportunity to make comparisons, so feel free to add in a few more.

- **DRIVING FORCES**: think of how the campaign came about – a tragic event? Politically motivated? Are individuals or organisations the key driving forces behind it? Is it a national or local campaign?
- **METHODS/MEDIA**: link together those who used similar methods and those who did not. Which campaigns used celebrities to endorse them and which did not? Social media? Newspapers and petitions?
- **SUCCESS**: compare the success of the campaigns for change. Which ones were successful? How do we know they were a success? Give examples of outcomes from the successful campaigns. Were some a partial success/ongoing? Use statistics or evidence where appropriate.

Remember, feel free to add other comparison points.

How to improve your comparison

Sample answer

Sample 1 – 'Purpose' paragraph

Purpose

Sarah's law involved a family who campaigned for legal changes regarding sex offenders. In 2000, Sarah Payne was abducted while playing with her siblings. She had been abducted and murdered by a man who lived close by, named Roy Whiting. A significant police search had started to find Sarah Payne, aged eight, and her mother and father were involved in several media conferences and on television, appealing for anyone to help find their daughter. Sarah Payne's body was found and it was confirmed that she was murdered. Roy Whiting was questioned shortly after her disappearance as he was on the Sex Offenders Register and he was eventually charged with her abduction and murder. Sarah's parents had started the campaign that information about sex offenders living in the area should be made available to allow parents to protect their children. There is a version similar in the US called Megan's law. The *News of the World* supported the campaign and ran a 'naming and shaming' campaign as well as a petition.

The purpose of this campaign was to change the law regarding sex offenders. The campaign aimed to introduce a policy/law to protect children; information about sex offenders living in the area should be available to parents to prevent any harm. The campaign was successful as it introduced the Child Sex Offender Disclosure Scheme. This campaign is similar to Clare's law, as this campaign also aimed to change the law. Clare's law involved a tragic event when a woman was violently murdered by her ex-partner. This campaign aimed to create a similar scheme where information about an individual's past could be disclosed to individuals. The purpose was for those entering new relationships to be able to find out if their new partner had a history of domestic abuse.

Commentary

This answer only covers the purpose of the campaigns (one comparison point only) and only includes reference to two campaigns. More importantly, the paragraphs are largely descriptive, with few comparisons. There is no need to describe the event or the campaign in this manner; this will only negatively impact time management.

The answer includes a number of accurate details regarding Sarah's law, followed by a clear explanation of the purpose and aim of this campaign for change. However, answers will be limited when descriptive, as the AC requires a 'comparative' skill. The comparison in this response has been highlighted. This is not sufficient for AC2.1 and the candidate would be expected to include a wider range of campaigns for change, more comparisons between various campaigns and to elaborate on these comparisons. Remember, the AC does not ask for a description.

Sample answer

Sample 2 – 'Purpose' paragraph

Purpose

Many campaigns had a similar purpose, that being to introduce a new policy or law or to amend an existing law. Sarah's law aimed to introduce a policy that enabled parents/guardians to find out the location of sex offenders from the police. Clare's law was very similar in that it aimed to introduce a scheme to allow individuals to find out if their partner had a history of domestic violence. However, some campaigns did aim to change existing criminal laws, rather than introducing a new policy or scheme. For example, Ann Ming aimed to change the law on double jeopardy whilst Lillian's law wanted to change the laws surround driving under the influence of drugs in order to make this stricter. Likewise, the assisted dying campaign aimed to encourage Parliament to change the law in order to make assisted dying legal.

On the one hand, the Brexit campaign differed from the previous campaigns. Brexit wanted to achieve a constitutional change to enable Britain to leave the European Union. This campaign differs considerably as it does not involve criminal law and the purpose is not based on the protection of individuals or rights.

Moreover, campaigns such as LGBT ones have many purposes. LGBT campaigns have campaigned to amend existing laws which fail to achieve equality such as gay marriage and adoption, etc. However, LGBT campaigns also aim to raise awareness of inequality to change social and political attitudes. Similarly, campaigns such as anti-smoking are not solely there to introduce smoking laws, such as no smoking in a public place, etc. Although this is a significant purpose of such campaigns, most anti-smoking campaigns such as those organised by the NHS or ASH are also there to raise awareness of the harmful effects smoking has.

This demonstrates that campaigns can have many different purposes. Most are there to introduce or change laws, whilst others also aim to raise awareness or change attitudes.

My campaign is similar to Clare's law as I aim to raise awareness of all forms of domestic violence, specifically male victims and the importance of recognising emotional abuse. My campaign could be regarded as similar to Clare's law due to the subject it concerns and the aim to prevent domestic violence. However, my campaign differs considerably from these campaigns as I do not wish to introduce or amend any laws.

Commentary

Although this response only compares the purpose of various campaigns (the first comparison point only), it is a considerably better response than the previous sample answer. This response includes eight different campaigns for change, as well as making an explicit comparison that links to the candidates' own planned campaign for change.

The response does not offer any irrelevant description and primarily focuses on comparisons, both similarities and differences between the purpose of various campaigns. The comparisons are clear and detailed with explicit reference to various campaigns to support conclusions. This is an excellent example of how to draw detailed comparisons for AC2.1. **This candidate would simply need to follow this same approach to draw comparisons on driving forces, methods and success to achieve very high marks.**

CHECKLIST – HAVE YOU INCLUDED:

- [ ] a clear and detailed comparison – similarities and differences about campaigns for change
- [ ] a range of relevant campaigns for change – minimum of five
- [ ] explicit links to your own planned campaign – compare your own planned campaign with existing campaigns? You may need to return to this and add this in once you have planned your own campaign in the next learning outcome.

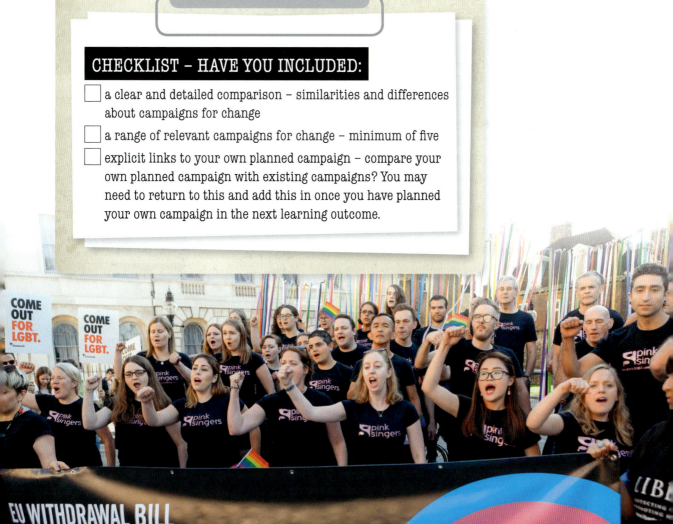

AC2.2 EVALUATE THE EFFECTIVENESS OF MEDIA USED IN CAMPAIGNS FOR CHANGE

See pages 55–62 of the textbook.

It's all about the evaluation

AC2.2 requires you to evaluate a range of media used in campaigns for change. 'Media' refers to:

- blogs
- viral messaging
- social networking
- advertising
- radio
- television
- film
- documentary
- word of mouth
- events
- print.

Events can be used to raise awareness and donations for campaigns for change.

In the controlled assessment you need to select a minimum of four different forms of media from the above list. You need to produce a clear and detailed evaluation of each media form you select, this includes: a brief definition and then detailed strengths and limitations of the particular media form.

However, to access the top mark band your answer requires 'clear evidence of well-reasoned judgements to support conclusions'. This means you need to include a real-life campaign in order to give your evaluative points some context. Select a campaign for change where the media form has been used effectively or ineffectively, and make sure you include evidence of how effective/ineffective it was – the numbers of tickets sold, the money raised from the event, the number of likes/shares on social media sites, etc. You must include this evidence for all media forms you select. The campaigns you choose do not need to be linked to crime and they do not need to be the same ones you considered in AC2.1. Any existing campaign for change that has used the media form will make it relevant.

Controlled assessment tip

Remember, you are not evaluating specific campaigns for change. You are evaluating how effective the media can be when used in campaigns for change.

This AC should be written in paragraphs, the use of a table or diagram will inevitably make your evaluation less detailed.

Pages 55–62 of the textbook include an evaluation of blogs, social networking, TV advertising, events, public appearances, merchandise and print leaflets. Pages 60–62 also include a sample answer marked as 10/15.

TV advertising

Activity 1.11

Develop your evaluation skills by watching the following television adverts on YouTube and answering the questions that follow below.

- 'Dogs Trust TV Ad #specialsomeone long version' (https://www.youtube.com/watch?reload=9&v=IrJhlVODG3w).
- 'THINK! Drink Drive: Photocopying #butalive' (https://www.youtube.com/watch?time_continue=14&v=2GgXckhOwCw).
- 'Right Now: Adyan Sings' (https://www.youtube.com/watch?v=DuJifOHISM8).

1. As a viewer, how does each advert make you feel while watching it?
2. How do the adverts attract the audience?
3. After watching the adverts do you feel you are more aware of the potential issue? Do you feel more inclined to donate? Why?
4. Was there anything particularly memorable about any of the adverts?
5. Was there anything in the adverts that could negatively affect the audience?
6. Have you seen these adverts before or are you more inclined to skip TV adverts?

Now it's time to evaluate the effectiveness of TV advertising when used in campaigns for change. After watching the adverts and answering the questions above, in pairs, write five strengths and five limitations of using TV advertising as a form of media in campaigns for change.

A second drink could double your chance of being in a fatal collision.

THINK!

#butalive

Strengths	Limitations

Activity 1.12

Summary table

Before you start writing this AC in paragraphs, it may be helpful to create a table similar to the one below for a range of media forms. This summary table may help you to organise your ideas, suggest strengths and limitations, and include relevant campaigns for change to use as evidence.

Method	Definition	Strengths/ Advantages/ Good points	Limitations/ Disadvantages/ Bad points	Real life campaign example
Example: blogs	Define the method briefly in the context of campaigns – what is a blog?	What are the advantages of using a blog in a campaign for change? (Aim for three developed points as a minimum.)	What are the disadvantages of using a blog in a campaign for change? (Aim for three developed points as a minimum.)	Make reference to a real-life campaign for change where a blog has been used effectively or ineffectively. How was it effective/ ineffective? Try to include evidence/ statistics.
Example: TV advertising				
Example: social networking				
Example: film				
Example: print leaflets				

Explore online

Now that you have developed your evaluation skills, you need to include an example of a real-life campaign where TV advertising has been used effectively, or even ineffectively.

Select a campaign for change featuring a television advert and use the internet to find some statistics you could use as evidence.

For example:
- How much money does Cancer Research UK raise each year? Could this be a result of its TV advertising?
- Do the 'THINK!' adverts raise awareness? Have the number of convictions for drink driving decreased? Could this be a result of the TV advertising?
- How much money does the Dogs Trust raise each year? How many dogs have been rehomed? Could this be a result of its TV advertising?

Helpful links:
- 'Cancer Research UK, Our Income' (https://www.cancerresearchuk.org/our-accounts-).
- 'THINK!, Welcome to THINK!' (http://think.direct.gov.uk/drink-driving.html).
- 'Dogs Trust, Success Stories' (https://www.dogstrust.org.uk/rehoming/success-stories/).

Dogs Trust uses TV advertising as a form of media.

CHECKLIST – HAVE YOU INCLUDED:

☐ a clear and detailed evaluation of the effectiveness of a range of media – minimum of four forms of media to be used

☐ relevant campaigns for change – providing evidence of the effectiveness/ineffectiveness of the media forms when used in real-life campaigns? This may include statistics if relevant.

Controlled assessment tip

Remember that a minimum of four media forms are to be included. However, this needs to be very detailed. If you are struggling to make well-developed points, it may be better to include five or six media forms.

LEARNING OUTCOME 3 PLAN CAMPAIGNS FOR CHANGE RELATING TO CRIME

AC3.1 PLAN A CAMPAIGN FOR CHANGE RELATING TO CRIME

See pages 63–69 of the textbook.

Now it's time to start planning your own campaign for change.

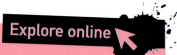

Need some inspiration for your own campaign?

Pathway Project works to support adults, young people and children, who are experiencing or affected by domestic abuse. (Pathway Project: https://www.pathway-project.co.uk)

Access Pathway Project's website and answer the following questions.
1. What under-reported crime is the focus of this project?
2. What are the key aims of this project?
3. What could the objectives of the project be?
4. Who is the target audience?
5. What methods are used by this project to raise awareness?
6. How is this project funded?

Stop Hate UK is one of the leading national organisations working to challenge all forms of Hate Crime and discrimination, based on any aspect of an individual's identity. (Stop Hate UK: https://www.stophateuk.org)

Access Stop Hate UK's website and answer the following questions:
1. What under-reported crime is the focus of this organisation?
2. What are the key aims of this organisation?
3. What could the objectives of the organisation be?
4. Who is the target audience?
5. What methods are used by this organisation to raise awareness?

There are many campaigns focused on challenging hate crime.

It is now time for you to start planning your own campaign for change relating to crime.

Use the planning table on pages 36–37 to organise your ideas and create a detailed plan. Remember, this AC is worth 10 marks so make sure you write in paragraphs, do not write the plan in a table during the controlled assessment.

Focus of your campaign	Your campaign must be linked to an under-reported or hidden crime. Typical examples include domestic abuse, hate crime, honour crime, technological crime, white-collar crime. Select a campaign focus based on a crime that you are most passionate about. Remember, your campaign for change does not need to link to the assignment brief.
Aims of your campaign	These are the overall or long-term goals. Typical examples include: • encourage victims to seek support for domestic abuse • raise awareness of the signs of violence within a relationship • educate and inform the public about hate crime.
Objectives of your campaign	These are the short-term plans that enable you to reach your aims. Typical examples include: • create a Twitter/Facebook account and achieve at least 600 re-tweets/shares or likes • create and display 50 posters in the town centre • create and distribute 150 leaflets to community centres in town • organise a fundraising event to raise £500 to be used towards producing merchandise.
Justification of your campaign	Why have you selected this particular under-reported/hidden crime? Are there any statistics to support the crime being under-reported? Are there any tragic events/cases linked to the crime? Keep this section of the plan brief, a detailed justification is provided in AC3.3.
Target audience of your campaign	Who is your target audience and why?
Methods to be used in your campaign	Which methods are you going to select? Select a minimum of three. Typical examples include: • posters, leaflets, merchandise, social networking pages, blogs, radio advertisements. Why have you chosen these particular methods? How are you going to use these particular methods in your campaign?
Materials to be used in your campaign	What materials will be needed to enable you to design and produce your methods selected above?

(Continued)

How you will fund your campaign	Financial planning includes the following considerations: • cost of materials • where these materials will come from • how many you will produce • overall cost • price sold for • profit • how the profit will be used • how the initial funds required to start the campaign will be raised.
Timescales for your campaign	Consider how much time will be allocated to each stage of the planning process: • research stage • design stage • creation of materials • implementation of the campaign. Be specific and realistic; for example, the research stage may take 4 weeks, whereas the time allocated to creating the materials may be 8–10 weeks.
Resources needed for your campaign	What general resources will be required for the campaign? Typical examples include: training, finance, materials, IT equipment, time, etc.

Remember, a detailed and appropriate plan is needed for mark band 3 (8–10 marks). Make sure your actions are appropriate, clearly described and in a relevant time sequence. The time sequence is very important to gain top marks.

Pages 67–69 of the textbook include an example of a financial plan as well as a step-by-step guide helping you to create a detailed time sequence. This may be helpful during your planning time.

CHECKLIST – HAVE YOU INCLUDED:

☐ a campaign for change linked to a crime that is under-reported or hidden

☐ a detailed and appropriate plan for change, including all of the key sections outlined by the WJEC specification (the sections can be found in the table on page 37 and above)

☐ clearly described actions, in a relevant time sequence?

Make sure your actions are in a relevant time sequence when planning the campaign, it is a key focus of this AC.

AC3.2 DESIGN MATERIALS FOR USE IN CAMPAIGNING FOR CHANGE

See pages 70–73 of textbook.

Now it's time to design your campaign for change.

Try to design a theme that can be used throughout to achieve consistency, that way your campaign will be more recognisable. This can be achieved by the use of a name, logo, colour scheme or particular images.

Explore online

Need some inspiration when it comes to designing materials?

In pairs, access the webpages to take a look at a range of materials used in existing campaigns for change. Address the two points below for all materials you look at:

1. Identify the key features that you think would be most effective in attracting attention from the audience.
2. Why are these features effective? (Consider: are they dramatic? Do they provoke an emotional response? Do they raise awareness by educating viewers? Etc.)

Materials

- Domestic violence increases during World Cup (poster shared via social media): Full Fact (2010–2018) 'World Cup: Does Domestic Abuse Spike When England Lose?' (https://fullfact.org/crime/world-cup-domestic-abuse/).
- Salvation Army poster – domestic violence – 'Why is it so Hard to See Black and Blue': Sam Rkaina (2015, 6 March) 'White and Gold Dress: Salvation Army Launches Powerful Campaign Against Domestic Violence Using "That Dress"', the *Daily Mirror* (https://www.mirror.co.uk/news/uk-news/white-gold-dress-salvation-army-5284119).
- Hate crime posters by Cheshire Police: Cheshire Constabulary (2018) 'Hate Crime Prevention Posters and Leaflets' (https://www.cheshire.police.uk/advice-and-support/hate-crime/hate-crime-prevention-posters-and-leaflets/).
- Honour crime poster: Louise Ridley (2015, 14 July) '"Honour Killing" Victim Shafilea Ahmed Remembered in Devasting Picture Reenacting Her Murder', Hufffington Post (https://www.huffingtonpost.co.uk/2015/07/14/shafilea-ahmed-honour-killings-uk_n_7793128.html?guccounter=1&guce_referrer_us=aHR0cHM6Ly93d3cuZ29vZ2xlLmNvbS8&guce_referrer_cs=IhrntkuyT_v5ruTzl83hwg).
- Women's Aid Twitter account (https://twitter.com/womensaid?ref_src=twsrc%5Egoogle%7Ctwcamp%5Eserp%7Ctwgr%5Eauthor).
- Stop Hate UK Facebook page (https://en-gb.facebook.com/Stop.Hate.UK/).
- Domestic violence – merchandise:
  - White Ribbon.org.uk (https://www.whiteribbon.org.uk/shop-landing/)
  - Café Press (https://www.cafepress.co.uk/+domestic-violence-awareness+gifts).

Controlled assessment tip

As this AC is worth 20 marks, you need to design a selection of materials to be used in the campaign for change that you planned in AC3.1. Design a minimum of three materials in order to access mark band 4 (16–20 marks). A minimum of three may include:
1. a poster
2. social media account (posts, comments, etc.)
3. merchandise (clothes, pens, cups, bags, etc.).

You may decide to create a fake Twitter account for your campaign.

After researching materials used in existing campaigns for change, it is now over to you to start planning the design of your very own materials. Remember, this part of the controlled assessment is an individual task and cannot be completed in pairs or groups.

Activity 1.13

Use the following table to organise your ideas, this will help you design the materials in your controlled assessment. The design features in the table are only suggestions, you may have your own ideas.

Merchandise can be effective in campaigns for change when trying to raise awareness.

Design ideas

Design feature	Your thoughts/ideas
Structure of information: • What is the most effective way to capture the attention of the audience – without causing confusion or giving them too much information? Consider layout/amount of text.	
Images: • Which images will you use? • How do these images link to your campaign? • Will the images capture attention? • Will you use a range of images or a consistent image across all materials?	
Persuasive language: • How will you promote change through your materials? • How will you encourage your audience to respond? • Will you talk directly to the audience? Consider phrases such as: 'you should', 'you don't deserve this', etc. • Will your language convey emotion?	

(Continued)

Design feature	Your thoughts/ideas
Promotion of action: • How will you promote action? Consider command words such as 'stop', 'ring now', 'get help now', etc.	
Target audience: • How will you target your audience? • Will the materials be relatable to that target audience? • Will the content be appropriate for that target audience? • How will you encourage your target audience to respond?	
Alignment with campaign: • How will you achieve consistency across the campaign? • Will your materials link? • How will they link? • Will you use the same logo, images or colour scheme, etc. for instant recognition?	
Final tip: • Remember to include helplines and/or contact information. • Will these be featured on all materials?	

Look at page 73 of the textbook to view a range of example materials designed by Criminology students.

CHECKLIST – HAVE YOU INCLUDED:

☐ well-designed and attractive materials – a minimum of three types

☐ appropriate content (materials) that will be suitable/effective for changing behaviour

☐ materials that are visually and verbally stimulating

☐ materials that are technically accurate?

AC3.3 JUSTIFY A CAMPAIGN FOR CHANGE

See pages 74–75 of the textbook.

Now it's time to justify your campaign for change

Now that you have planned and designed your campaign for change, you must justify your actions. Make sure you justify your entire campaign in this AC, not simply the materials you designed as part of AC3.2.

Key term

Justify: explain with good reasons what you have done and why you have chosen to do it.

Writing frame

You could use the writing frame below to help structure your justifications. This AC is worth 15 marks and should be written in clear and detailed paragraphs.

Justify your campaign choice

Justify your decision for selecting this under-reported/hidden crime. It is time to persuade the public why this campaign for change is needed. This is where you present a case for action.

- **What evidence is there that your crime is under-reported?**

You should include statistics that highlight the issue of the crime being under-reported.

Also include a real-life case example here. This case example could be used to stress the effects of the under-reported crime on victims or the lack of awareness of it in society. This will give you the opportunity to persuade people that your campaign is necessary and therefore justified. This section will provide evidence in support of your planned campaign.

Include statistics to support your evidence.

- **What impact will your campaign for change have?**

What impact are you hoping to achieve with your campaign for change? Is it necessary? Will it be successful? You may need to refer to your aims in AC3.1 here. Were you hoping to increase awareness, educate or inform the public, raise awareness regarding support available? Also, consider existing campaigns for change; if you were inspired by the success of an existing campaign, then that can be used as evidence to persuade people that your campaign will also be successful.

- **What would happen if you hadn't created this campaign for change?**

Remember, you need to use persuasive language here as this is where you persuade people that your campaign is truly justified. Consider the position without a campaign like this. Would society still lack awareness? Would people still be reluctant to report crimes or seek support?

Justify your key features

Justify the key features within your campaign for change. Remember, you must use persuasive language throughout to persuade others that your campaign is purposeful.

- **Name of campaign**

Why did you choose this name? Does it appeal or link to your target audience? Is it clear regarding the focus of the campaign? Does it link to the aims?

- **Logo**

Have you chosen a specific logo to use? Does this achieve consistency throughout all campaign materials, ensuring the audience becomes familiar with your campaign? Why have you chosen that logo? Is it a powerful image? What is the meaning behind it? Did you gain inspiration from any other existing campaigns for change?

- **Hashtags**

Have you created a hashtag linked to your campaign for promotion and advertisement on social media? Why have you created it? Does it raise awareness? Will it attract attention?

- **Tag line/slogan**

Have you included a tag line or slogan? If so, why? Will it encourage people to react to your campaign? Does it use persuasive or emotive language?

- **Colour scheme**

Do you have a consistent colour scheme? If so, why? Will this appeal to the target audience? Do the colours represent anything linked to the crime/campaign?

- **Other key features**

Have you used any other unique features throughout your campaign to raise awareness or attract attention? This may be a helpline or celebrity endorsement, etc.

Justify your chosen methods

Justify the methods and materials you have designed. This is where you should use evidence in support of a case.

- **Range of methods**

Justify your reasons for selecting the methods (poster/social media/ merchandise, etc.). Why did you select this range of methods? Will these methods attract your target audience? Will these methods reach

A hashtag may be used to encourage trending on social media.

Key terms

Tag line: a catchy or short, snappy statement that usually promotes action or persuades the audience to do something or think a particular way.

Slogan: a short and memorable phrase often used for the purpose of advertising.

a wider audience? Are these methods more appropriate in terms of achieving your aims? Did you select these methods due to cost? You should be including evidence or statistics here to support your decisions; for example, if Twitter was used due to the wider audience it attracts, then include statistics of social media usage. Or, if you opted for posters as opposed to leaflets for the benefit of a younger target audience, why? Also, consider existing campaigns for change; if you were inspired by the success of an existing campaign, then that can be used as evidence to persuade people that your campaign methods will also be successful.

Remember, you can refer to pages 74 and 75 of the textbook for sentence starters to help you write this justification.

- **Images**

Have you included imagery on your materials? If so, why did you opt for those images? Will the images appeal to the target audience? Are you using shock tactics? Are the images powerful or will they cause an emotional response?

- **Persuasive text**

Have you used persuasive language or text throughout the materials? If so, why have you chosen these phrases/terms? What meaning do the terms convey? Will they convince the audience?

- **Layout/fonts**

Have you designed the materials using a particular layout? Why? Why have you chosen that font or size of font? Is it to attract attention?

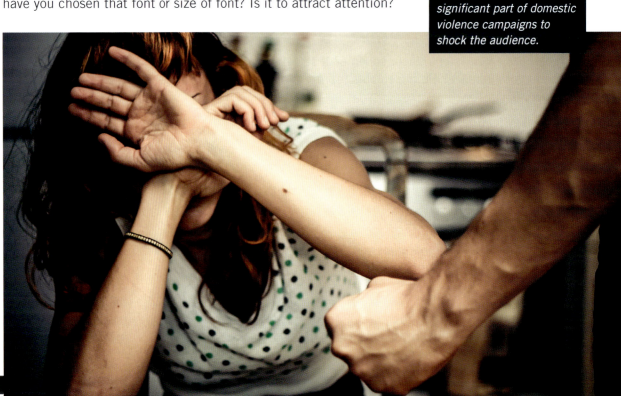

Imagery can be a significant part of domestic violence campaigns to shock the audience.

Activity 1.14

Read the paragraph below. This paragraph only addresses the first section of AC3.3, a justification of the campaign choice.

How would you improve this paragraph?

I chose to focus on domestic violence as my campaign for change because it is an under-reported crime in Britain. Most people are aware of domestic violence, yet simply do not know the true extent to which it occurs. For this reason, I think it is an important area to address as awareness needs to be raised and victims are in need of support. Without a campaign like this, it is likely that more victims would suffer from domestic violence with little help from agencies as they are too scared to report it. My aim is therefore to encourage women to report violence. Hopefully, with my campaign more women will seek help and people will be more aware of the signs of an abusive relationship.

CHECKLIST – HAVE YOU INCLUDED:

☐ a clear and detailed justification that is well reasoned

☐ conclusions that are supported by relevant judgements, including the use of persuasive language

☐ key justifications as outlined above? This may cover: reason for campaign choice, name, logo, methods, colour scheme, persuasive text, images, etc.

UNIT 2
CRIMINOLOGICAL THEORIES

AC1.1 COMPARE CRIMINAL BEHAVIOUR AND DEVIANCE

See pages 74–83 of the textbook.

Summary of crime and deviance

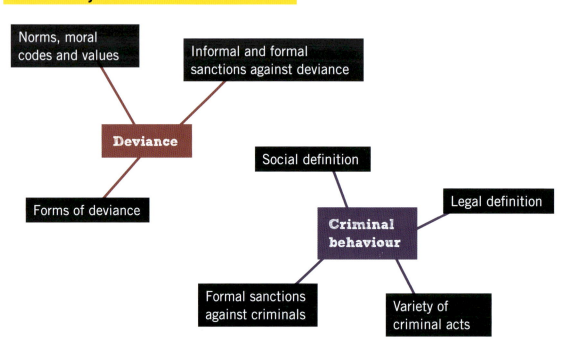

Norms, moral codes and values

Informal and formal sanctions against deviance

Deviance

Forms of deviance

Social definition

Legal definition

Criminal behaviour

Formal sanctions against criminals

Variety of criminal acts

Crime and deviance

It is important to be able to compare crime with deviance and appreciate not only when they are the same but also when they are different.

Criminal behaviour only	Deviance only	Criminal behaviour and deviance
Acts that break the rules, deemed to be illegal by the law-making powers of a society. For example, murder or assault. Such acts result in punishment by the police (such as a caution) or by a court (such as a fine or imprisonment).	Acts that are against social norms. For example, shouting in a library or cross-dressing. Such acts result in sanctions from others in society such as name calling or ignoring the deviant person.	Some crimes can be against social norms and are therefore deviant such as theft or fraud but crimes such as speeding and illegal downloading of music are sometimes so commonplace that they are not deemed to be considered deviant.

Key terms

Compare: explain similarities and differences.

Crime: breaches of rules set as criminal by a society.

Deviance: acts against social norms.

Why crime and deviance are so difficult to define

Crime can vary from one society to another, so what may be a crime in the UK is not necessarily a crime in another country. For example, marrying a 14-year-old child is illegal in the UK but acceptable in the state of Utah in the USA. In other words, if a society says an act is a crime then it becomes one. But not all societies can agree on what a crime should be. A legal definition would mean a crime has an *actus reus* and a *mens rea*. However, crimes of strict liability do not need a *mens rea*.

Deviance is usually defined as going against the norms of a society. However, the norms (values and mores or moral codes) can vary between different societies and can vary at different times. For example, in many countries it is the social norm to wear black clothing to a funeral but the typical colour to a Buddhist funeral is white. Smoking cigarettes was once considered sophisticated and was encouraged, even by the medical profession. However, today it could be considered wrong, anti-social and even deviant.

It is also important to be able to identify both deviance and criminal behaviour from a scenario.

The words crime and deviance are difficult to define.

Key terms

Actus reus: a guilty act.

Mens rea: a guilty mind.

Example questions

Read the following question from the **Unit 2 2018 exam paper**:

Edna and Sidney are neighbours. Edna is obsessed with cats and has 40 of them in her house. She has lived in poverty for many years. Sidney is a wealthy, elderly punk rocker who always dresses in punk rocker clothes and styles his hair in a spiked multi-coloured mohawk. He also regularly illegally downloads music and plays it at high volume late at night. Edna and Sidney intensely dislike each other and regularly argue. Edna complains about the music and Sidney calls Edna 'a crazy old woman'. Many of their neighbours shout abuse at Edna saying she is mad and needs locking up. Edna has never complained to the police about this. One night she found graffiti on her door saying 'mad woman'. When she heard Sidney's music she went to his house armed with a kitchen knife, and stabbed him in the heart. He died shortly after the attack.

Using examples from the scenario, explain behaviour that could be described as criminal, deviant or both. [5 marks]

Sample answers

Answer A

Listening to loud music is a deviant behaviour as it's not really breaking any laws but society looks down on it. A crime has occurred when Edna stabbed Sidney. The vandalism on Edna's door could be classed as both a crime and deviant.

This answer is worth **3/5**. There are three examples of actions from the text: one being deviant, one being criminal and the final example is both. There is some attempt at giving an explanation for the classifications. However, more examples from the text and more detailed reasoning for the classifications would increase the marks.

Sanctions against crimes = prison, fines and community orders such as probation.
Sanctions against deviance = name calling, ignoring someone and laughing at someone.

Exam tip ✔

In an exam it is wise to read the question and scenario at least twice to be familiar with the content. It is also acceptable to write anything you need to on the question paper or underline key points. You are also able to write a short plan or answer structure.

Exam tip ✔

The exam question above contains many examples of crime and deviance. To provide a 5 mark answer it is important to include a large number of those examples with comparisons between the two terms.

Answer B

The behaviour from the scenario which would be seen as criminal would be Sidney illegally downloading music, the graffiti on Edna's door and the murder of Sidney. Things that would be seen as deviant would be Sidney playing loud music and possibly the way he dresses and styles his hair. Also, Edna having 40 cats may be seen as deviant as well. The criminal behaviour goes against written laws but it would also be seen as deviant by going against social norms.

This answer is worth **4/5**. Several actions from the text are included in the answer and there is reasoning for the classification of acts. All three types of classifications are included. The answer could be improved, as shown in answer C below.

Answer C

Deviant behaviour goes against social norms and hence the following would be considered deviant: keeping 40 cats, dressing as an elderly punk rocker with a multi-coloured mohawk and playing loud music late at night. On the face of it none of these actions are criminal, merely deviant. However, crimes are breaches of the criminal law set by a society and would include the murder of Sidney, the graffiti on Edna's door, name calling and the illegal downloading of music. Some of these actions could be considered both criminal and deviant, namely graffiti, the murder of Sidney and the name calling from neighbours. The illegal downloading of music is criminal but is arguably common in society and may not be classed as deviant.

This answer is worth **5/5**. It has a large number of examples from the text and explains why the actions are criminal and deviant. In addition, the comment on downloading music shows the difference between the two terms.

Exam tip ✔

An exam question may ask for examples and if this is the case make sure you put them in. However, it is also a good idea to add in examples, even if not specifically asked for, to provide detail and development to your answer.

Activity 2.1

Complete the word search on 'crime and deviance'.

N	S	K	M	M	D	A	D	Y	Y	X	Q	J	S	J
V	O	M	I	W	E	H	H	U	M	U	X	T	U	K
S	K	I	R	W	K	N	A	S	H	M	B	D	E	U
W	I	C	T	O	Z	I	S	B	V	X	I	Y	R	P
R	C	U	X	I	N	O	I	R	V	C	H	K	S	B
G	C	M	Z	X	N	E	N	S	E	P	C	V	U	L
Q	O	T	T	I	O	I	N	W	A	A	Q	G	T	L
Y	M	J	F	Z	U	O	F	I	D	Y	S	Z	C	A
A	P	Y	Z	S	I	O	L	E	I	G	G	N	A	G
Z	A	D	M	T	Q	V	Q	D	D	Q	B	C	D	E
V	R	B	C	Q	A	H	N	V	A	F	O	I	S	L
S	E	N	N	L	M	F	K	D	T	P	C	A	Q	N
U	A	V	U	V	J	L	L	F	O	W	M	P	H	O
S	C	E	B	H	G	W	H	E	K	E	M	I	R	C
I	S	K	O	B	E	D	E	V	I	A	N	C	E	T

Words to find:

ACTUS REUS
COMPARE
CRIME
DEFINITION
DEVIANCE
LEGAL
MENS REA
NORMS
SANCTIONS
VALUES

Exam tip

This AC focuses on the word 'compare'. Go to pages 188–189 of this book for advice on how to interpret this word and answer an exam question with it in.

Test yourself

1. Can you state three sanctions to deviance?
2. Can you state three sanctions to criminal behaviour?
3. Discuss if smoking cigarettes is deviant or criminal behaviour.
4. Give three examples of behaviour that could be classed as both deviant and criminal.

CHECKLIST – ARE YOU ABLE TO:

☐ define the word crime

☐ define the word deviance

☐ explain why the words crime and deviance are difficult to define

☐ compare crime and deviance

☐ state sanctions against criminal behaviour and deviance

☐ select both the criminal behaviour and deviance from a scenario and explain your reasoning?

AC1.2 EXPLAIN THE SOCIAL CONSTRUCTION OF CRIMINALITY

See pages 84–89 of the textbook.

How laws change from culture to culture

How laws change over time

Social construction

How laws are applied differently according to circumstances in which actions occur

Why laws are different according to time, place and culture

Exam tip ✔

This AC can be summarised along the lines of 'a crime is a crime because society classes it as one'. Sometimes, the view of society will change over time, in different places or within different cultures. As a result of this, what is considered a crime will also change.

Culture

At any one time, the law in one culture may be very different from the law in another culture.

Can you think of any cultures different from your own?

Here are some ideas:

Laws vary in different cultures.

- Laws in Pakistan reflect the Muslim culture of this country. For instance, homosexuality is illegal, as is cohabitation by an unmarried couple. Possession of even small quantities of illegal drugs can lead to imprisonment. The death penalty can be imposed for crimes such as blasphemy, murder and rape. The cause of the differences between Pakistan and the UK law is due in part to the religious values and beliefs of the country.

- The different culture between the USA and the UK can also lead to different laws. For example, in many American states you have to be 21 years of age to buy alcohol, whereas in the UK it is generally 18.

Synoptic link

Think back to Unit 1 and honour crimes. These types of crimes are popular and acceptable in some cultures.

See pages 21–22 in the textbook.

Key terms

Culture: the ideas, customs and social behaviour of a particular people or society.

Moral crimes: crimes against morality, often considered to be victimless crimes because there is no specific victim.

Explore online ←

Explore laws from Afghanistan by looking at the article on the Human Rights Watch website about moral crimes in Afghanistan: 'Afghanistan: Surge in Women Jailed for "Moral Crimes"' (2013, 21 May) (http://www.hrw.org/news/2013/05/21/afghanistan-surge-women-jailed-moral-crimes).

Consider why women are treated in this way and why it is most unlikely to occur in England and Wales.

Time

As time goes by, laws have changed as a result of a changing society. A changing society needs different laws to reflect its views and moral codes.

Can you think of any laws that have changed in your lifetime?

Over time, society changes its view and morals.

Activity 2.2

From your own knowledge or research, complete the following table regarding laws in England and Wales since 1950. Give brief details of the changes.

	1950's laws	Modern laws
The selling of cigarettes		
Capital punishment for the offence of murder		
Minimum wage laws		
Homosexuality		

Take it further

Research the theme of domestic abuse in society. Consider how, as society has changed, laws have also changed to prevent abuse happening. This research can also be used to show the social construction of criminality.

Key term

Social construction: something based on the collective views developed and maintained within a society or social group.

Place

Just because there is a law in one place doesn't mean that it will be the law in another. As societies are different, so too are the rules which they say should be the basis of criminal law.

Activity 2.3

Attempt the following quiz, selecting the appropriate answer(s) – some may have more than one.

1. Jaywalking (crossing the road without regard to traffic regulations) is an offence in which country?
   (a) Most urban states of the USA
   (b) England and Wales
   (c) Canada
   (d) Singapore

2. According to the law in India, a girl cannot marry before what age?
   (a) 14
   (b) 16
   (c) 18
   (d) 21

3. Adultery is illegal in which of the following places?
   (a) England and Wales
   (b) Saudi Arabia
   (c) Arizona, USA
   (e) Kansas, USA

4. Female genital mutilation is practised in which countries?
   (a) Somalia
   (b) Chad
   (c) Kenya
   (d) Egypt

5. Until recently, which country had a one-child policy and would fine parents if they had more children?
   (a) Japan
   (b) Ethiopia
   (c) Germany
   (d) China

As societies vary in different places so too do the laws of those societies.

Jaywalking is not a crime in the UK but it is in other parts of the world.

Test yourself

Answer this question from the **Unit 2 2017 exam paper** and then compare your answer with the example answer found online.

With reference to examples, analyse how laws change due to time, place and culture. [9 marks]

Final point on this AC

Laws are applied differently according to the circumstances in which they occur.

Activity 2.4

See page 89 of the textbook.

Using the textbook as your guide, complete this activity by adding in the missing words.

While everyone is subject to the same law as the age of _____ _____ in the UK is ten, anyone committing a crime under this age will not be _____, charged or _____.

In England and Wales if someone is charged with murder the law allows an alternative charge of _____ where a person has suffered _____ responsibility or has a _____ of control. Hence, the circumstances in which these crimes have occurred will result in different treatment.

The age for criminal responsibility in the UK is ten years but in Botswana it is 14 and in Kenya it is eight.

CHECKLIST – ARE YOU ABLE TO:

- [ ] explain the term social construction of criminality
- [ ] explain, with examples, how laws change over time
- [ ] explain, with examples, how laws change in different places
- [ ] explain, with examples, how laws change in different cultures
- [ ] explain at least one circumstance where laws are applied differently?

LEARNING OUTCOME 2 KNOW THEORIES OF CRIMINALITY

AC2.1 DESCRIBE BIOLOGICAL THEORIES OF CRIMINALITY

See pages 90–95 of textbook.

This full unit is called 'Criminological Theories', which is broken down into three categories:

- biological
- individualistic
- sociological.

Key terms

Biological: relating to processes or activities concerned with living things. For our purposes it relates to the body, both inside and outside, as reasons for committing crimes.

Genetic: relating to genes or heredity.

AC	Category of theories	Sub-category	Name of theory	Summary of theory
2.1	Biological	Genetic	XYY	An extra Y chromosome in men may produce extra testosterone and lead to aggression and criminality.
			Twin studies	Identical twins (MZ) are more likely to have concordance (be similar) than non-identical (DZ) – supporting genetics (nature) causing crime.
			Adoption studies	If an adopted child is more like their biological parents, from a criminal viewpoint nature rather than nurture may be responsible for crime.
		Physiological	Lombroso	Criminals are those with atavistic (primitive) features.
			Sheldon	The mesomorph somatotype is most likely to be criminal.
		Other biological theories	Brain abnormality	Damage to the frontal lobe cortex of the brain may cause individuals to be criminals.
			Neurochemicals	Chemicals ingested may impact on people's actions and feelings. For example, serotonin or steroids.

Notes: DZ = dizygotic; MZ = monozygotic

XYY syndrome

See pages 90–91 of the textbook.

Test yourself

To ensure you understand the XYY theory, answer the following:
1. What is XYY?
2. How is this linked to criminality?
3. What is the name of the researcher linked to this syndrome?
4. What does her research say?
5. Name two people linked to the XYY theory.

XYY Syndrome

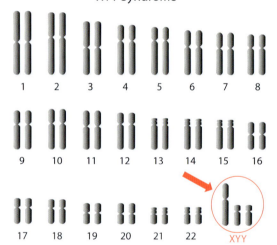

XYY is linked to aggression and criminality.

Exam tip ✓

Marks are often not achieved in an exam for writing about the wrong theory. For example, where a 5-mark question asks you to describe a biological theory you will receive zero marks for describing an individualistic or sociological theory. It is therefore vital that you appreciate the biological categories as outlined in the table on page 55.

Exam tip ✓

Do not focus too much on symptoms of XYY that do not relate to criminality. For example, men with XYY are often taller than average in height. This does not relate to why they commit crime. Instead, focus on the increased aggression and possible criminality as a result of it.

Twin studies

Twins can be identical (monozygotic or MZ) or non-identical (dizygotic or DZ).

▼

MZ twins share 100% of their DNA; DZ twins share 50% of their DNA.

▼

If MZ twins have a higher concordance rate, then nature rather than nurture will be key.

▼

Christiansen (1977) studied 3,586 twins from the Danish islands and found concordance rates of 35% for MZ and 13% for DZ for male twins, and 2% for MA and 8% for DZ female twins.

Explore online

Watch the following video on YouTube and make notes on the research carried out in the Scottish hospital and on Richard Speck, a murderer who was thought to have XYY syndrome:
• 'The Myth of the "Supermale" and the Extra Y Chromosome' (https://www.youtube.com/watch?v=6BsXLn Ln9ok&t=4s).

Adoption studies

Adoption studies allow a comparison of criminals with their biological and adoptive parents. Where a criminal is raised by non-biological parents:

| If the criminal is similar to their natural parents | ▶ | a genetic basis for criminality is suggested (nature). |
| If the criminal is similar to their adoptive parents | ▶ | an environmental basis for criminality is suggested (nurture). |

Adoption studies look at the nature versus nurture argument.

RESEARCH

Hutchings and Mednick ('Registered Criminality in the Adoptive and Biological Parents of Registered Male Criminal Adoptees', in Fieve et al., *Genetic Research in Psychiatry*, 1975) studied 4,000 adopted children and found a high proportion of boys with criminal convictions also had biological parents with convictions.

Mednick et al. ('Prenatal Influenza Infections and Adult Schizophrenia', *Schizophrenia Bulletin*, 1975, 20(2), 263–267) found no relationship between criminal convictions of adoptive parents and convictions of adopted children.

Activity 2.5

Be the examiner. Write your own exam-style scenario involving either a twin or adoption situation. Ensure that there is some criminality that can be attributable to either the twin or adoption theories.

Take it further

Read the following article and produce a summary argument in support of Stephen Mobley's appeal case:

- Steve Connor (1995, 12 February) 'Do Your Genes Make You a Criminal?', the *Independent* (https://www.independent.co.uk/news/uk/do-your-genes-make-you-a-criminal-1572714.html).

Physiological theories

The two physiological theories are those credited to Lombroso and Sheldon.

See pages 92–94 of the textbook.

Key term

Physiology: the functions of living organisms, in our case human beings and their parts, and, in particular, the way in which they function.

Activity 2.6

Using the textbook to help, write a summary of each theory. There are some important terms you must include.

Important terms: separate species, born criminal, atavistic, somatotype, mesomorph, endomorph, primitive, ectomorph

LOMBROSO

SHELDON

Cesare Lombroso

Example questions

Past exam questions concerning these two theories, from **Unit 2 2018** (first) and **Unit 2 2017** (second) **exam papers**, are as follows:

- *Describe one physiological theory of criminality. [5 marks]*

- *With reference to the text above, describe the main features of one physiological theory of criminality. [6 marks]*

Activity 2.7

Consider the following sample answer to the first example question on the previous page and, using the mark scheme below, consider how many marks you would give the answer. If you do not award it full marks, what do you believe is missing?

Describe one physiological theory of criminality. [5 marks]

Lombroso's theory stated that criminality was inherited. You could tell who was a criminal by looking at them. The atavistic features such as sloping foreheads or enormous jaws. He believed criminals were not fully evolved and were homo-delinquents.

Physiological theories have appeared on the exam paper.

0 marks: Nothing worthy of any marks.

1–3 marks: Answers that describe in limited detail **one** physiological theory of criminality. Answers convey meaning but lack detail. Little or no use of specialist vocabulary.

4–5 marks: Answers that describe in detail **one** physiological theory of criminality. Answers clearly communicate meaning with some use of specialist vocabulary.

Sheldon

Activity 2.8

Write a paragraph describing Sheldon's theory using this picture.

Ectomorph   **Mesomorph**   **Endomorph**

Sheldon's theory of somatotypes states that mesomorphs are more likely to be criminal.

Test yourself

Can you answer the following questions?
1. What is meant by 'atavistic'?
2. Can you give examples of atavistic features?
3. Who argued that the physical shape of the head and face determined the 'born criminal'?
4. If you have thick lips and protruding ears, which offences could you be guilty of?
5. What do Sheldon's and Lombroso's theories have in common?
6. What is the shape of an endomorph?
7. What are the characteristics of an ectomorph?
8. According to Sheldon, which body type is least likely to be a criminal?
9. Murderers are likely to have what characteristics?
10. According to Sheldon, which body type is most likely to be a criminal?

This AC also links to AC4.1 'Assess the use of criminological theories in informing policy development'. This means the theories considered are used as the basis of policies to prevent crime occurring. In other words the theories can help suggest ways to control crime.

Other biological theories

Finally, there are other biological theories, including that of brain abnormality and the use of neurochemicals such as serotonin.

See pages 94–95 of the textbook.

Activity 2.9

Prepare a mind map for each of the following:
(i) brain abnormality and (ii) neurochemicals.

Example questions

Typical exam questions would include:
- *Describe a biological theory of criminality.*
- *Describe a genetic theory of criminality.*
- *Describe a physiological theory of criminality.*
- *Describe a biological theory referred to in the text.*

CHECKLIST – ARE YOU ABLE TO:

☐ describe a genetic theory of criminality (including XYY, twin and adoption studies)

☐ describe a physiological theory of criminality (including Lombroso and Sheldon)?

AC2.2 DESCRIBE INDIVIDUALISTIC THEORIES OF CRIMINALITY

AC	Category of theories	Sub-category	Name of theory or theorist	Summary of theory
2.2	Individualistic	Learning theories	Bandura	Criminality is like any other behaviour in that it can be learned through observation and positive or negative reinforcement, e.g. the bobo doll experiment.
			Sutherland	Differential associations theory: when different learning takes place from different people or associations. Criminality can be learned.
		Psychodynamic theories	Freud	Focuses on early childhood experiences and feelings of guilt, and our unconscious mind. This can result in criminality. The psyche is divided into the Id (selfish and animalistic urges), the Ego (seeks rational and sensible control) and the Superego (the moral conscience). Conflicts between the three can result in criminality.
			Bowlby	Maternal deprivation thieves study. Those separated from their mothers are more likely to turn to criminality.
		Psychological theories	Eysenck	Certain personalities are more likely to be criminal: the extrovert/neurotic and psychotic personalities.

Note: the theorists mentioned in the table above are the ones identified in the specifications. Other theorists may be studied instead and will be credited in an exam situation, provided they address the exam question.

Exam tip ✔

Marks are often not achieved in an exam as a result of writing about the wrong theory. For example, where a 5-mark question asks you to describe an individualistic theory you will receive zero marks for describing a biological or sociological theory. It is therefore vital that you appreciate the individualistic categories as outlined in the table above.

Key term

Individualistic: relating to an individual rather than society as a whole.

Bandura and social learning theory

See pages 96–99 of the textbook.

See pages 96–99 of the textbook.

Take it further

Read the following article and make brief notes about the research linked to the learning theory:

· Keith Perry, and agency (2014, 10 September) 'Watching Violent Films Does Make People More Aggressive Study Shows', *Telegraph* (https://www.telegraph.co.uk/news/science/11087683/Watching-violent-films-does-make-people-more-aggressive-study-shows.html).

Activity 2.10

Using the information in the textbook, write a summary of Bandura's social learning theory (SLT). Below is a list of important terms that should be included.

Important terms: observational learning, positive reinforcement, negative reinforcement, bobo doll, Bandura, aggression, role model, imitate

You could also add information about Sutherland's differential associations theory to support Bandura's learning theory. Check your answer against the sample on page 99 of the textbook.

Freud's theory of criminality

See pages 100–101 of the textbook.

Activity 2.11

Complete the crossword below on Freud's theory of criminality.

Across

3. This is your moral conscience.
5. Criminals are those with this as an undeveloped part of their personality.
6. This type of life experience can have a major impact on criminality.
9. The complex where sons have sexual feelings for their mother.
10. The part of your mind that is hidden, rather like the majority of an iceberg.
12. Freud's first name.
13. This acts as the mediator between the Id and Superego.

Down

1. Feeling of this is often linked to criminality.
2. An individual who is Id dominated is more likely to be this.
4. If you are Id dominated you want instant ....?
7. He carried out a study of 44 thieves.
8. Freud's work is an example of this type of theory.
11. The rational and sensible part of the personality.

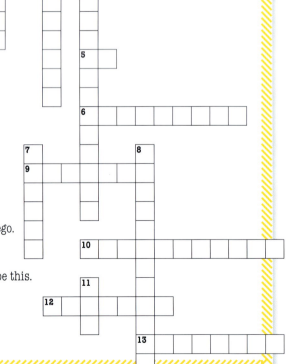

Eysenck's psychological personality theory

See pages 101–102 of the textbook.

Below is a diagram showing the types of personalities used by Eysenck in his theory of criminality.

Activity 2.12

Indicate on the diagram the type of personality that is most likely to be criminal. Also add in the dimension of psychoticism that Eysenck later added to this personality model.

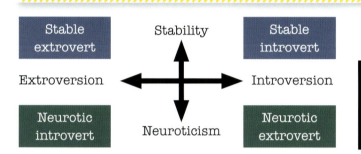

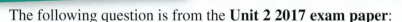

Eysenck's theory of criminality is linked to the personality.

Take it further

Research the case of Nick Leeson, known as a rogue trader at Barings Bank, then answer the following:

1. Briefly explain his crime.
2. Decide which type of personality he may have.
3. Apply Eysenck's personality theory to his criminality.

Example question

The following question is from the **Unit 2 2017 exam paper**:

Paul, an unemployed local man, has been convicted of murder. He was convicted after getting into a fight with Ian over an allegation of theft of money. Paul also has numerous previous convictions for drug dealing and theft. He has been in care since the age of seven after his parents were given long custodial sentences. Ian's father, a local barrister, has started a campaign to bring back capital punishment for crimes of murder. His campaign has attracted the attention of local media and politicians.

Describe any one individualistic theory of criminality. [5 marks]

For the above question any individualistic theory could be used. However, the best thing to do is read all the other questions before you attempt to answer this one. Often you will be asked to go on to analyse the theory you write about in this part question regarding the scenario involving Paul. You may also have to evaluate the theory too. Therefore, armed with this knowledge you can select the most appropriate theory that can be used to answer all the questions.

Take it further

Can you think of a scenario where a criminal's personality could be identified in accordance with Eysenck's theory of criminality? Try to link the way the crime is committed to the personality traits.

Activity 2.13

Following are three answers describing three different theories that could all be used to answer the question on the previous page about Paul. Read the answers and, using the mark scheme, decide the marks that you would award each one.

Sample answers

Theory 1 – psychodynamic theory

One theory is the psychodynamic theory, where Freud believes all humans have criminal urges that are repressed in the unconscious mind. These feelings can be controlled by the Superego (the morality principle) which develops during childhood. If a childhood trauma occurs, such as maternal deprivation, it could disrupt its development. This could mean the Id is then able to become the dominant part of the personality. The Id is the pleasure-seeking principle. Therefore, Freud believes crime is a result of an underdeveloped Superego. This theory is backed up by Bowlby's 44 thieves study.

Sigmund Freud

Theory 2 – social learning theory

One individualistic theory is the social learning theory. This theory by Bandura states that all behaviour is learned as a child as we observe role models who are usually the same gender as us and older than us and we imitate their behaviour. Bandura did an experiment using a bobo doll to see if the children imitated the aggressive behaviour they observed the adults perform to prove this theory. The results of the experiment showed the children copying the role models and they even developed some of the violent behaviour.

John Bowlby

Albert Bandura

Theory 3 – psychological personality theory

One individualistic theory comes from Eysenck who put forward the view that a person's personality is a major contributor as to whether or not they commit crime. Eysenck broke the personality down into three parts: extroversion, neuroticism and psychoticism. Taking Eysenck's personality test determines a person's score in each of these three parts. He suggested that people who scored highly in psychoticism and extroversion were more likely to be criminal.

0 marks: Nothing worthy of any marks.

1–3 marks: Answers that describe some aspects of one individualistic theory of criminality. Answers convey meaning but lack detail. Little or no use of specialist vocabulary.

4–5 marks: Answers that describe in detail one individualistic theory of criminality. Answers communicate meaning with some use of specialist vocabulary.

Exam tip

To help with your revision always consider the mark scheme. The one to the left focuses on the detail provided. For example, mark band 1–3 refers to 'some' detail but the 4–5 mark band is reserved for answers that contain detail. Also note the importance of specialist terminology. This can make the difference between marks and mark bands.

Test yourself

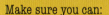

Make sure you can:
1. Explain the bobo doll experiment and how it can relate to criminality.
2. State who are likely to be our role models.
3. Name the main theorists connected to the various theories.
4. Include an explanation of differential associations.
5. Explain the characteristics of the Id, Ego and Superego.
6. Explain how Bowlby's research links to the psychodynamic theory.
7. State and explain all the dimensions of personality in Eysenck's theory of criminality.
8. Use specialist terminology such as observational learning, instant gratification, unconscious mind, extroversion, introversion, neuroticism, stability and psychoticism.

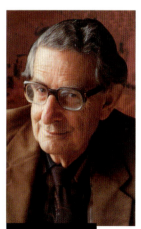

Hans Eysenck

CHECKLIST – ARE YOU ABLE TO:

☐ describe a learning theory of criminality

☐ describe a psychodynamic theory of criminality

☐ describe a psychological theory of criminality?

AC2.3 DESCRIBE SOCIOLOGICAL THEORIES OF CRIMINALITY

See pages 103–107 of the textbook.

Exam tip

Marks are often not achieved in an exam as a result of writing about the wrong theory. For example, where a 5-mark question asks you to describe a sociological theory you will receive zero marks for describing a biological or individualistic theory. It is therefore vital that you appreciate the sociological categories as outlined in the table below.

Key terms

Bourgeoisie: the middle and upper classes who own the means of production in industry.

Proletariat: the lower social class, who must provide their labour to the upper classes for a wage.

AC	Category of theories	Sub-category	Name of theory or theorist	Summary of theory
2.3	Sociological	Social structure	Marxism	The upper class or bourgeoisie use crime as a way of controlling the lower class or proletariat. Police, etc. focus on the crime of the lower class as they believe they are the cause of crime.
			Merton's strain theory	Robert Merton suggested society sets goals to achieve but not everyone can reach them using legitimate means. Those who cannot may become an innovator and use crime to achieve material success.
		Interactionism	Labelling	Crime is a social construction. Howard Becker suggested that if society labels an act as criminal it will be considered to be criminal. The self-fulfilling prophecy will result in a person acting as a criminal.
		Functionalism	Émile Durkheim	Crime is inevitable and serves a function or purpose in society as long as it is the right amount. It will bring society together and allow social cohesion.

(Continued)

AC	Category of theories	Sub-category	Name of theory or theorist	Summary of theory
		Realism	Right	Has its roots in political conservatism and links to a lack of social bonds. According to Charles Murray, the 'underclass' are more likely to commit crime due to their weak social restraints.
			Left	A capitalist society creates crime due to its inequalities. So, individuals are motivated by consumerism and may turn to crime to seek what they cannot afford.

Note, most of the theorists mentioned in the table above are the ones identified in the specifications. Other theorists may be studied instead and will be credited in an exam situation provided they address the exam question.

Social structure theory – Marxism

Key term

Criminogenic: causing or likely to cause criminal behaviour.

Bourgeoisie & proletariat

A capitalist society produces unfavourable conditions for the lower class, e.g. unemployment

Ruling class use crime as a way to control the lower class

Karl Marx was a German philosopher who developed the theory of communism

Agents of social control such as the police focus on the working class and encourage them to conform

Capitalism is criminogenic as it encourages criminal activity

Crimes committed by the upper class, e.g. white-collar crimes, are usually ignored

Governments fabricate crime statistics to suit their own purposes, including the desire to get public support to supress the working classes

Merton's strain theory

See page 105 of the textbook.

According to Merton's strain theory, society promotes the idea of the American dream, with material success being the goal. When the goals cannot be reached, people will feel the strain, or anomie as termed by Merton. However, not everyone will accept that these goals are appropriate for them and may, for instance, rebel against society and set their own goals. Some people, however, may not be able to achieve the goals through legitimate means but still have the desire to reach the dream. These individuals may use illegal means to get what they want. These people are most likely to be criminal and are termed 'innovators' by Merton.

The table below explains Merton's theory and how individuals adapt to anomie.

Key terms

American dream: the idea of equal opportunity for all to achieve high aspirations and goals.

Anomie: loss of shared principles or norms.

Adaption by the individual as defined by Merton	Definition	Accepts means	Will seek to reach approved goals	Likely to commit crime	Examples from the **Explore online** task below
Conformist	Accepts approved goals and pursues them through approved means.	Yes	Yes	No	
Innovator	Accepts approved goals but uses disapproved means to achieve them.	No	Yes	Yes	
Retreatist	Abandons approved goals and approved means.	No	No	Yes	
Ritualist	Abandon's society's goals but will conform to approved means.	Yes	No	No	
Rebel	Challenges approved goals and approved means.	No – replace	No – replace	Yes	

The strain theory revolves around achieving the American dream.

Explore online

Watch the 'Merton Strain Theory' video on YouTube (https://www.youtube.com/watch?v=fvVd9oOxTm8) and include examples of each of the adaptions in the table above.

Interactionism

Labelling

Howard Becker put forward the labelling theory as a way of explaining criminality. It focuses on how we interact with each other and the idea that crime is a social construction. If someone is labelled as criminal, they will behave in ways that reflect the label placed upon them. The process of labelling someone makes the individual both deviant and criminal. This causes negative repercussions, as society will be biased against them because of the label. The individual becomes a self-fulfilling prophecy by taking on the label and being criminal becomes their master status.

HELLO
I AM
what you label me

Labelling, according to Howard Becker, can explain criminality.

Example question

Following is one of the questions on the **Unit 2 2018 exam paper**:

Edna and Sidney are neighbours. Edna is obsessed with cats and has 40 of them in her house. She has lived in poverty for many years. Sidney is a wealthy, elderly punk rocker who always dresses in punk rocker clothes and styles his hair in a spiked multi-coloured mohawk. He also regularly illegally downloads music and plays it at high volume late at night. Edna and Sidney intensely dislike each other and regularly argue. Edna complains about the music and Sidney calls Edna a 'crazy old woman'. Many of their neighbours shout abuse at Edna saying she is mad and needs locking up. Edna has never complained to the police about this. One night she found graffiti on her door saying 'mad woman'. When she heard Sidney's music she went to his house armed with a kitchen knife, and stabbed him in the heart. He died shortly after the attack.

(a) *Describe a sociological theory of criminality. [4 marks]*
(b) *Analyse how the theory described above can be applied to Edna's situation. [5 marks]*

Part (a) of the question requires a short description of the theory and part (b) requires the theory to be broken down and applied to Edna.

There are several sociological theories that could be used to answer the above questions. One of them could be the labelling theory. This is because of the name calling that Edna has received from her neighbour Sidney and other people in the area. She is called a 'crazy old woman', 'mad' and 'needs locking up'. Thus, Edna reacts by fulfilling these labels and becomes a criminal by killing Sidney.

Exam tip ✔

An exam question could refer to:
 (i) a sociological theory
 (ii) a social structure theory
 (iii) a theory covering interactionism
 (iv) a realism theory.

Functionalism

See page 105 of the textbook.

Activity 2.14

Revise functionalism by answering the following questions.

1. Who states that crime is inevitable?
2. Why is crime inevitable?
3. If crime is functional, when does it become dysfunctional?
4. Why is it bad for there to be too little crime? Include an example.
5. Why is it bad for there to be too much crime?
6. What does 'anomie' mean?
7. What does this phrase mean: 'crime strengthens social cohesion'?
8. What does the phrase 'boundary maintenance' mean?
9. Give an actual example of boundary maintenance.
10. Who argued that crime/deviance can act as a 'warning light' (you may have to research this answer)?

Realism

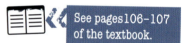

See pages 106–107 of the textbook.

Right and left realism provide contrasting ideas of the causes of crime. Basically, right realism asserts that criminals make a choice to commit crime. Whereas left realism suggests that the impact of society, in particular relative deprivation on communities, causes criminal behaviour.

Key term

Relative deprivation: how someone feels in relation to others or compared with their own expectations.

Right or left realism?

Activity 2.15

The following are statements that apply to either left realism or right realism. Allocate them to the right direction.

		Right	Left
A.	Comes from political conservatism.	☐	☐
B.	Focuses on being tough on crime.	☐	☐
C.	Inequalities are created by a capitalist society.	☐	☐
D.	Charles Murray supports this theory.	☐	☐
E.	Seeks practical solutions to the causes of crime.	☐	☐
F.	Criminals lack social bonds.	☐	☐
G.	A more equal and caring society is needed to reduce crime.	☐	☐
H.	The underclass are responsible for crime.	☐	☐
I.	Supports reducing criminality by prevention and use of things such as closed-circuit television (CCTV) and zero tolerance.	☐	☐
J.	People do not have the power or resources to fully participate in society and are therefore marginalised.	☐	☐
K.	Crime can be reduced by improving leisure facilities for the young.	☐	☐

Take it further

Read the article called 'Left and Right Realism' (http://www.julianhermida.com/contrealism.htm) and make a list of specialist terminology that can be added to your notes on left and right realism.

Exam tip

The exam question is likely to be very general and ask you to 'Describe a sociological theory of criminality'. Make sure whichever theory you select you relate it to the reason for people committing crime.

CHECKLIST – ARE YOU ABLE TO:

☐ describe a social structure theory of criminality (includes Marxism and strain theory)

☐ describe interactionism (includes the labelling theory)

☐ describe functionalism

☐ describe left and right realism?

Exam tip

In an exam every Learning Outcome must be tested. However, not every AC must appear on the exam paper.

LEARNING OUTCOME 3 UNDERSTAND CAUSES OF CRIMINALITY

AC3.1 ANALYSE SITUATIONS OF CRIMINALITY

See pages 108–114 of the textbook.

Exam tip ✔

Each exam paper will contain three questions with each one having its own scenario or information about criminality. This AC requires you to apply your knowledge of the specification to the scenario or text. Each scenario will contain information about criminal behaviour and there will be clues that point towards reasons why that behaviour is committed. This in turn will link to criminological theories.

The exam question will be worded along the following lines: 'Analyse the theory described above to X's situation.' X is the person named in the scenario.

Key term

Analyse: examine in detail, break into component parts, examine relationships.

The exam question will be a scenario involving criminal behaviour.

Example question ?

Paul, an unemployed local man, has been convicted of murder. He was convicted after getting into a fight with Ian over an allegation of theft of money. Paul also has numerous previous convictions for drug dealing and theft. He has been in care since the age of seven after his parents were given long custodial sentences. Ian's father, a local barrister, has started a campaign to bring back capital punishment for crimes of murder. His campaign has attracted the attention of local media and politicians.

The above scenario is from the **Unit 2 2017 exam paper**. You will also find it on page 63 of this book under AC2.2. There we considered the question:

*Describe any **one** individualistic theory of criminality. [5 marks]*

However, this time we need to consider the next part of the question, namely:

Analyse how the theory described above can be applied to Paul's situation. [5 marks]

Exam tip ✔

Make sure you analyse the theory described in the first question otherwise zero marks will be awarded. This is why it is important to read all the questions following a scenario before you attempt to answer any of them.

Make sure you're familiar with the exam structure.

Sample answers

We will now consider three answers to the question on the previous page, using the following mark scheme.

0 marks: Nothing worthy of any marks.

1–3 marks: Answers that analyse some aspects of how an individualistic theory of criminality described above can be applied to Paul's situation. Answers convey meaning but lack detail. Little or no use of specialist vocabulary.

4–5 marks: Answers that analyse in detail how an individualistic theory of criminality described above can be applied to Paul's situation. Answers communicate meaning with some use of specialist vocabulary.

Answer 1 (Bandura's theory)

This theory could be applied because his parents do not really care about Paul as they left him at the age of seven when they were given long custodial sentences. Paul grows up just like his parents when he gets into fights and drug deals. This shows he has learned from his parents.

This would receive **2/5** as it touches upon the idea of imitation but is limited in detail and analysis. Much more could be added, including more detail from the scenario, for example the fact that Paul has been in care and may have learned criminality from his peer role models in the care home.

Answer 2 (Bandura's theory)

Paul's parents were criminals as they were given long custodial sentences. When Paul was young he saw this and has modelled his behaviour on his parents. As Paul's parents broke the law, this taught Paul to break the law too. Paul has copied his parents by modelling himself on them.

This would receive **3/5** as the detail is again limited but does convey the core of the theory by applying it to Paul's situation. There is also slightly better terminology in this answer compared with the first one.

Exam tip ✔

Try to add detail in an exam answer by developing the point you are making. Use specialist terminology wherever possible and add in examples to support your answer.

Exam tip ✔

To help prepare you for the exam, try answering previous exam questions.

Answer 3 (Bandura's theory)

Paul has been in care since the age of seven when his parents were given long custodial sentences. In his childhood, Paul's parents were engaged in criminal behaviour, which he imitated because of their modelling. His parents were the source of his observational learning. Paul is also said to have numerous previous convictions for drug dealing and theft, which supports this approach in that he has learned directly from his parents' behaviour. Also, his time in the care home may have influenced his behaviour, especially if he received positive enforcement from his actions such as money for selling the drugs. Like the children in the bobo doll experiment, he seems to have evolved further into criminal behaviour by murdering Ian.

This would receive **5/5** as the analysis is detailed and conveys an accurate understanding of the theory. There are also several specialist terms used in the answer. It could be further enhanced by the addition of Sutherland and differential associations to support the application.

Example question

We have already seen the scenario below on page 69, when we looked at AC2.3 and the sociological theories.

Edna and Sidney are neighbours. Edna is obsessed with cats and has 40 of them in her house. She has lived in poverty for many years. Sidney is a wealthy, elderly punk rocker who always dresses in punk rocker clothes and styles his hair in a spiked multi-coloured mohawk. He also regularly illegally downloads music and plays it at high volume late at night. Edna and Sidney intensely dislike each other and regularly argue. Edna complains about the music and Sidney calls Edna a 'crazy old woman'. Many of their neighbours shout abuse at Edna saying she is mad and needs locking up. Edna has never complained to the police about this. One night she found graffiti on her door saying 'mad woman'. When she heard Sidney's music she went to his house armed with a kitchen knife, and stabbed him in the heart. He died shortly after the attack.

(a) *Describe a sociological theory of criminality. [4 marks]*
(b) *Analyse how the theory described above can be applied to Edna's situation. [5 marks]*

Exam tip ✓

Try to use as much of the scenario as you can to explain why the crime has occurred. Do not leave anything out.

SCENARIO

There will be three scenarios or passages of information in each exam unit.

Sidney is an elderly punk rocker.

Sample answers

We will look at two different answers to the analysis question. Use the mark scheme below to decide the mark that you would give it.

0 marks: Nothing worthy of any marks.

1–3 marks: Answers that analyse some aspects of how the sociological theory of criminality described above be applied to Edna's situation. Answers convey meaning but lack detail. Little or no use of specialist vocabulary.

4–5 marks: Answers that analyse in detail how the sociological theory of criminality described above can be applied to Edna's situation. Answers communicate meaning with some use of specialist vocabulary.

Answer 1 (Marxism)

Edna is a proletarian due to living in poverty and Sidney is bourgeois as he is rich and upper class. Due to Edna being proletariat, people abuse her because she is low in society's eyes.

This answer would receive **2/5**. While the detail is limited there is an attempt at using specialist terminology. However, there is no link between criminality and the theory.

Answer 2 (Marxism)

Marxist theory can apply to Edna's situation as she lives in poverty. Therefore, she is forced into crime as she becomes desperate and believes the bourgeoisie agencies such as the police will not help her. She may have felt she needed to take it upon herself to murder Sidney as the only way to stop the problems, as he was wealthy so may have been part of the bourgeoisie.

This answer would receive **4/5** as there is a detailed attempt at analysing and applying the theory to Edna's situation. There is also an obvious link between the theory and reason for criminality. To improve this answer further there could be a link to more facts from the question such as Edna not reporting the harassment to the agents of social control.

> **Exam tip** ✔
>
> You should note that an exam mark scheme will also give an idea of what is expected in an exam answer. It is not a model answer but is only brief details of the expected content.

> **Exam tip** ✔
>
> You are advised to spend approximately one minute per mark on the exam questions. So, if a question is worth 5 marks, you should spend approximately five minutes answering it. This is because the exam lasts 90 minutes and is worth 75 marks. This would allow 15 minutes overall or five minutes per main question to plan and check an answer.

Activity 2.16

Now write a 5/5 answer to the Edna and Sidney question (b) on page 74, using any other sociological theory.

You be the teacher and write your own exam scenarios.

Take it further

Pair up with a friend and each one of you should write your own exam questions. Try to write three scenarios, one focusing on a biological theory, one using an individual theory and one centred around a sociological theory. Then swap and answer each other's questions.

Note
Right and left realism take a very political view of crime.

Key term

Politics: the activities linked to the governance of a country

CHECKLIST – ARE YOU ABLE TO:

☐ analyse all theories and apply all theories to a scenario

☐ read and use all the facts in a question, relating them to the relevant criminological theory?

AC3.2 EVALUATE THE EFFECTIVENESS OF CRIMINOLOGICAL THEORIES TO EXPLAIN CAUSES OF CRIMINALITY

See pages 114–121 of the textbook.

Evaluation is a key skill that is highly likely to appear in the exam. It could follow on from a previous question. Can you remember the Sidney and Edna situation from the **Unit 2 2018 exam paper**? See page 77 of this book.

Three of the questions following the scenario are:

1. *Describe a sociological theory of criminality. [4 marks]* – AC2.3
2. *Analyse how the theory described above can be applied to Edna's situation. [5 marks]* – AC3.1
3. *Evaluate the effectiveness of the sociological theory described above in explaining causes of criminality. [6 marks]* – AC3.2

You can see that the third question is evaluative in nature, and would mean you evaluate the same theory you selected to describe and then analyse in the previous questions. This is another reason why you need to carefully select the theory in the first question – to ensure you are also able to evaluate it.

Evaluation means that you need to judge something, and this often means to consider the strengths and weaknesses of a theory (or theories). It is very important to remember that the evaluation in this instance is how effective the theory is in explaining why people commit crime. So, it is not about the theory itself and whether you believe it is a good theory. For instance, your political views may lie in communism and follow those of Marx. However, you are not deciding if it is a good political opinion but rather whether the theory is effective, or not, at explaining the reason for criminality.

Key term

Evaluate: to what extent do you agree with the theory? Make a judgement about the quality or importance of a theory by providing strengths and weaknesses of how well the theory supports the reason for criminality. Ideally, come to a conclusion and justify how you have made your choice.

Evaluation is an important skill that is likely to appear in the exam paper.

Exam tip ✔

In the exam an evaluation question may be in the form of a single theory, as above in the Sidney and Edna situation. Or a group of theories may need to be evaluated. For example, in the **Unit 2 2017 exam paper** the following question was asked:

Evaluate the effectiveness of a range of individualistic theories to explain causes of criminality. [8 marks]

Make sure that when you evaluate you comment on both strengths and limitations of the theory, otherwise you will not achieve full marks.

The question that asks you to evaluate will not expect you to also describe the theory. The description of the theory will be in a different question. So, when you evaluate, go straight into the strengths or limitations. DO NOT explain the theory otherwise it will be a waste of precious exam time.

Evaluation phrases

The phrases below will lead you into evaluating:

- A strength of this theory is …
- The theory endeavours to show …
- However, a limitation is …
- On the other hand …
- A further strength is …
- A principal concern with the theory is …
- A supporting factor is …
- Criminality is linked to …
- This theory is supported by …
- However, nothing in the theory explains …
- This supports the contention that …
- Despite this, it could be argued that …
- Conversely, this also …
- A key strength is …
- The theory does not substantiate …
- This idea is corroborated by …

Evaluation requires both positive and negative points in an answer.

Activity 2.17

With the help of the phrases above and your knowledge of sociological theories, write an answer to this question:

> Evaluate a range sociological theories in explaining criminality.

Note: where a range of theories is required at least three should be included.

Exam tip ✔

Remember you could be asked to evaluate one theory or a range of theories from the biological and/or individualist and/or sociological ACs. Therefore, you should revise them all.

Activity 2.18

This activity relates to the evaluation of three biological theories. You need to match the Evaluation point to the Theory – Lombroso, Sheldon or the XYY theory – in the table on the following page. Also decide if the point is a strength or weakness. Your answers can be checked using the textbook, pages 116–118.

Exam tip ✔

It is important to appreciate how to evaluate as this skill also appears in Units 1, 3 and 4.

Evaluation point	Theory	Strength or weakness?
Charles Goring (1913) did find a low-order intelligence in convicts, which suggests some genetic basis to criminality.		
Focusing too heavily on genetics ignores the behaviourist approach.		
A number of other studies have confirmed that there is a small association between body build and criminality (Putwain & Sammons, 2002).		
Does not take into account that people's somatotype is not fixed. People's bodies change throughout their lives.		
Adler et al. (2007) indicated that it is possible aggressive and violent behaviour is at least partly determined by genetic factors.		
Several pieces of research, e.g. Bath Spa University (Butcher & Taylor, 2007), suggest that less attractive individuals are more likely to be considered guilty.		
Scientific racism – DeLisi (2012) – indicated that many of the atavistic features defined are specific to people of African descent.		
Could not really explain how ectomorphs and endomorphs can also be criminals.		
A good-sized sample (200) was used and, importantly, this theorist used a control condition of non-offenders (students) to compare the results to.		
Not everyone with atavistic features is a criminal and not all criminals have them.		
However, studies have found that genetic abnormalities are widespread throughout the general population and therefore do not explain aggression.		
Even though there could be issues surrounding the reliability of this study, other researchers have found results that seem to support, at least in part, the initial theory. Glueck and Glueck (1956) found in their research that, in a sample of delinquents, 60% were mesomorphs, while in a non-delinquent sample there were only 31%.		
Consider if mesomorphs get picked upon or invited/dared to do illegal acts? Because of the way people consider mesomorphs, they may be drawn into delinquent activities by peer groups.		
Lack of a control group – so no comparisons can be made.		

Sample answers

Consider the following question from the **Unit 2 2017 exam paper** and sample answers, and, using the mark scheme below, decide the appropriate mark.

Evaluate the effectiveness of a range of individualistic criminological theories to explain causes of criminality. [8 marks]

0 marks: Nothing worthy of any marks.

1–3 marks: Answers that evaluate with limited/basic detail the effectiveness of a range of individualistic criminological theories to explain causes of criminality. Answers convey meaning but lack detail. Little or no use of specialist vocabulary.

4–6 marks: Answers that evaluate with some detail the effectiveness of a range of individualistic criminological theories to explain causes of criminality. Answers communicate meaning with some use of specialist vocabulary.

7–8 marks: Answers examine with detail the effectiveness of a range of individualistic criminological theories to explain causes of criminality. Answers are well structured and clearly expressed. Specialist terms are used with ease and accuracy.

Answer A

One individualistic criminological theory is the social learning theory. This is where behaviour is observed then copied by the observer. This could be a cause of criminality because if someone has observed criminal behaviour they could pick it up and do it themselves. For example, if someone observed their father hitting their mother they might pick it up and do it themselves believing it to be appropriate. This is effective because it has been proved to be true by the bobo doll experiment. Another theory is the psychodynamic theory. This is all about the Id, Ego and Superego. It argues that if one of these isn't developed enough it can be an answer as to why people are criminal. It can be effective in the way that it is scientific but is from a long time ago.

Exam tip ✓

Evaluation is a higher order skill and a question may ask you to evaluate more than one theory. If you are asked to evaluate a range of theories make sure you include at least three different ones. This will help you reach the top mark band.

Take it further »

Can you improve the wording within this answer? For example, improve the specialist terminology with phrases such as 'observational learning', and rather than 'pick it up' use the word imitate. In addition, use the phrase 'substantiated by the bobo doll experiment' rather than 'proved to be true'.

Answer B

Freud's theory can be criticised because it can't be scientifically proven due to the theory being based on the subconscious mind. This is a weakness because if a theory can't be scientifically proven then it can't be viewed as a reliable theory. The only thing that could be scientifically tested was the treatment. However, this was unsuccessful and so the theory is not very effective in explaining criminality. Eysenck's theory of criminals having high levels of extrovertism, neuroticism and also psychoticism as personality traits can be criticised because an individual's personality is not stable. Your personality changes depending on certain events in your life, therefore the test may state you have a criminal personality when really you may have just experienced a traumatic event in your life. Therefore, the test is not effective because it only measures your current personality. However, the theory can be more scientifically proven than Freud's psychodynamic theory. The behaviourist theory can also be criticised because, although it has scientific laboratory-based research, the research does not relate to crime in a real-life setting and therefore lacks **ecological validity**.

SCIENTIFIC METHOD

If a theory has scientific support it will be classed as a main advantage when evaluating the theory.

Take it further

Can you develop the final evaluation point on the behaviourist theory, as stated in the answer on the left?

Key term

Ecological validity: the extent to which the findings of a research study are able to be generalised to real-life settings.

CHECKLIST – ARE YOU ABLE TO:

- [ ] evaluate all biological theories
- [ ] evaluate all individualistic theories
- [ ] evaluate all sociological theories?

LEARNING OUTCOME 4 UNDERSTAND CAUSES OF POLICY CHANGE

AC4.1 ASSESS THE USE OF CRIMINOLOGICAL THEORIES IN INFORMING POLICY DEVELOPMENT

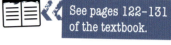

See pages 122–131 of the textbook.

This AC requires you to consider ideas that have been created from the criminological theories. The ideas or policies consider crime control and can be both formal and implemented as laws or rules and informal or unofficial ideas that may be followed but are not compulsory. Usually, the formal policies are implemented by the government.

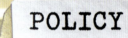

Activity 2.19

Here is a list of formal and informal policies that have been developed from ideas linked to the criminological theories. Can you insert them into the correct column of the table below?

- custodial sentence
- detention in school
- community orders including probation
- curfews
- withholding of pocket money
- grounding by parents
- fines
- cognitive behaviour therapy.

The policies in this AC are all linked to the criminological theories.

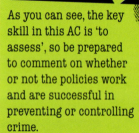

Exam tip

As you can see, the key skill in this AC is 'to assess', so be prepared to comment on whether or not the policies work and are successful in preventing or controlling crime.

Formal policies	Informal policies

Individualistic theories informing policy development

Activity 2.20

Read the exam-style scenario below, then answer the question that follows.

Example question

Glenn, aged 20, has been involved in crime since the age of ten when his parents separated and he went to live with his grandmother. Initially stealing from local shops, his criminal behaviour has become more serious and he is now involved in drug dealing. Glenn is a very angry young man who also has three convictions for assault occasioning actual bodily harm (ABH).

Assess relevant individualistic policies which may be appropriate to prevent Glenn from committing further criminal offences.
[7 marks]

Biological theories informing policy development

Neurochemicals

Activity 2.21

Using your knowledge of the effects of neurochemicals in food, design a menu for meals at a Young Offenders Institution. Try to plan meals using foods that have a positive and calming effect on the prisoners.

Key term

Neurochemicals: chemicals which can transfer signals that can regulate thoughts and emotions.

Basal ganglia

Thalamus

Hypothalamus

Amygdala

Raphe nuclei

Raphe nuclei

Cerebellum

Serotonin can positively influence aggressive behaviour and is found in foods such as eggs, salmon, turkey, nuts and seeds.

Eugenics

Explore online

Watch the YouTube video 'Mad Science: Eugenics and Selective Breeding' (https://www.youtube.com/watch?v=gWur8Rbc3hc) and answer the following questions:

1. What is meant by the phrase 'modern dog breeds are genetically disconnected from their ancient ancestors'?
2. Other than dogs, what has been used for selective breeding?
3. Why have plants and crops been genetically modified?
4. Who termed genetics to mean 'born well'?
5. How was eugenics considered in the late 19th and early 20th century?
6. What are the modern views on eugenics?

Key terms

Eugenics: the science of improving a population by controlled breeding, to increase the occurrence of desirable heritable characteristics.

Capital punishment: also known as the death penalty, is the legally authorised killing of someone as punishment for a crime.

Capital punishment

See page 126 of the textbook.

Take it further

1. Read 'Is the Death Penalty a Deterrent?' on the Death Penalty Information Center website (https://deathpenaltyinfo.org/study-88-criminologists-do-not-believe-death-penalty-effective-deterrent), an American site, then make notes and use statistics to decide if the death penalty is a deterrent to crime.

2. Watch 'Capital Punishment is Still Practised in One European Country. Which is it?' a video on YouTube by *The Economist* (https://www.youtube.com/watch?v=TND3V3cS5iw) and use some of the comments to write a list of reasons why the death penalty should be abolished.

Capital punishment is the most extreme biological way of controlling crime.

Sociological theories informing policy development

See pages 127–131 of the textbook.

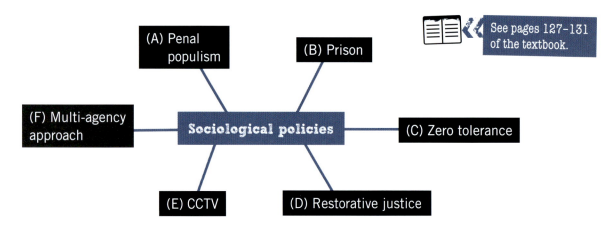

(A) Penal populism

(B) Prison

(F) Multi-agency approach

Sociological policies

(C) Zero tolerance

(E) CCTV

(D) Restorative justice

Activity 2.22

The statements below relate to one of the sociological policies named in the mind map on the previous page. Using the textbook, where all the statements can be found, match each statement to the correct policy, using the letters from the diagram on the previous page.

1. It is one of the first requests made by the police at the start of their enquiries. ☐
2. The government's attempts at proposing laws to punish offenders that will be popular with the general public. ☐
3. For example, issues such as safeguarding or domestic abuse may be prevented. ☐
4. The strategy is based on the 'broken windows' theory, developed by George Kelling and James Wilson. ☐
5. Is a voluntary process involving the person who has suffered harm and the person who has caused harm. ☐
6. One of the main ways society tries to control crime. ☐

The use of CCTV is a major investigative technique.

Key term

Inform: to give knowledge or have an impact/effect.

CHECKLIST – ARE YOU ABLE TO:

☐ understand what is meant by the phrase 'assess the use of criminological theories in informing policy development'

☐ give examples of formal policies

☐ give examples of informal policies

☐ assess the use of biological theories in informing policy development

☐ assess the use of individualistic theories in informing policy development

☐ assess the use of sociological theories in informing policy development?

AC4.2 EXPLAIN HOW SOCIAL CHANGES AFFECT POLICY DEVELOPMENT

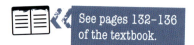

See pages 132–136 of the textbook.

This AC relates to society and how the views of people can change and, as a result, laws or policies also change. There is a link to AC1.2 Unit 2 but the focus there is how different societies or cultures have different laws; whereas, the focus of this AC is how a policy develops within the same society.

Synoptic link
The public perception of crime allows a synoptic link to Unit 1 AC1.5, pages 38–42 of the textbook.

Social values, norms and mores

The table on page 87 that shows the differences between the above terms and includes modern examples that could also be used in an exam answer on this topic.

Exam tip ✔

An exam question will not ask you to discuss specific laws such as smoking, homosexuality or women's rights. However, these are the type of laws that will allow you to answer a more general question from this AC. The wording of an exam question in this area could include the following terminology:

- social values, norms and mores
- public perception of crime
- structure of society
- demographic changes
- cultural changes.

As society changes, so too does the law.

CHANGE

	Definition	Example	Modern example of policy development
Social values	Rules shared by most people in a society, or ideas that they hold in value. They are more general guidelines than norms.	Most people feel we should respect the elderly.	**Cannabis oil**: cannabis is currently a controlled drug, as classified by the Misuse of Drugs Act 1971. However, in July 2018, Home Secretary Sajid Javid announced that specialist doctors in the UK will be able to legally prescribe cannabis-derived medicinal products.
Norms	Social expectations that guide behaviour and explain why people behave and act in the way they do. They keep in check deviant behaviour. It is expected behaviour but could vary from one culture to another.	For instance, in the UK, dark, sombre colours are usually worn to funerals but in China the colour of mourning is white.	**New psychoactive substance/ legal highs**: the chemicals, sold under names such as spice and black mamba, which are designed to give users the same effect as drugs like cannabis and cocaine, were legal until the Psychoactive Substances Act 2016.
Mores	Mores are good ways of behaving. Norms that a culture would think of as too serious to break.	For example, murder	**Upskirting**: the taking of surreptitious, sexually intrusive photographs. It is to become a specific criminal offence punishable by up to two years in prison in a government Bill introduced into Parliament in June 2018.

Example question

The **Unit 2 2017 exam paper** included the following question:

Discuss how social changes can affect policy development. [8 marks]

The type of information that would go into an answer is as follows on page 88.

The type of information that would go into an answer is as follows on page 88.

Take it further

Research the current position on the prescription of cannabis oil-based products, noting in particular the limited conditions for which it is likely to be prescribed. It is suggested that you read 'Medical Cannabis (and Cannabis Oils)' on the NHS website (https://www.nhs.uk/conditions/medical-cannabis/).

Death penalty

- In the 18th century, society approved of the death penalty as it protected the upper classes and their property. However, as time passed it was restricted to those guilty of murder or treason.
- Further changes resulted in temporary abolition for murder in 1965.
- Permanent abolition for murder in 1969, but it remained for treason until 1999 due to the European Convention of Human Rights.
- Miscarriage of justice cases such as Derek Bentley and Timothy Evans swayed public opinion.

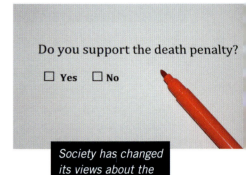

Do you support the death penalty?

☐ Yes ☐ No

Society has changed its views about the death penalty.

Domestic abuse

- Social change concerning the position and status of women in society. For example, at the beginning of the 20th century women had very few rights; however, in 1918 they obtained the right to vote.
- Rule of thumb – allowed a man to beat his wife with a stick so long as it was no thicker than his thumb.
- Legal attitudes changing over time. Cases such as *R* v *R*, which established the possibility of marital rape.
- Policing attitudes changing over time from a laissez-faire attitude to the establishment of specialist Domestic Violence Units. This was followed by legislation in 1996 (the Family Law Act) and in 1997 (the Protection from Harassment Act).
- Numerous anti-discrimination laws.
- Domestic Violence Disclosure Scheme (Clare's law).

See page 86 of the textbook for details of the Derek Bentley case and page 200 for the Timothy Evans case.

See page 142 of the textbook for more on Clare's law.

The law on domestic abuse has changed significantly over the past 50 years.

Assisted suicide

- Suicide was originally a crime and a mortal sin, which meant the denial of a Christian burial.
- Change in social policy when it was decriminalised by the Suicide Act 1961.
- Assisted suicide is still a criminal offence, punishable with up to 14 years in prison.
- Introduction of 'guidelines' by the Director of Public Prosecutions (DPP) to indicate when a prosecution is likely and unlikely. Reference to the Debbie Purdy case.
- Proposals to legalise assisted suicide have failed. Most recently, Lord Falconer's 'Assisted Dying Bill'.

Synoptic link

To Unit 1 and campaigns for change.

Demographic changes

Criminologists use demographics to understand the reasons why crime occurs, the location of crime and who commits it. Aspects of demographics such as age, race, gender and social class can be studied to provide information on criminal behaviour.

Synoptic link

The statistics provided for demographic changes can link to Unit 1 AC1.6 'Evaluate methods of collecting statistics about crime', pages 43–45 of the textbook.

Demographics can help explain criminality.

Example question

The **Unit 2 2018 exam paper** asked the following question:

Explain how social values, norms and mores may impact on policy development. [7 marks]

Using the mark scheme below, decide how many marks you would award Answer B on the next page.

0 marks: Nothing worthy of any marks.

1–3 marks: Answers explain with limited detail how social values, norms and mores may impact on policy development. Answers convey meaning but lack detail. Little or no use of specialist vocabulary.

4–6 marks: Answers explain with some detail how social values, norms and mores may impact on policy development. Answers communicate meaning with some use of specialist vocabulary.

7 marks: Answers explain with detail how social values, norms and mores may impact on policy development. Answers are well structured and clearly expressed. Specialist terms are used with ease and accuracy.

Key term

Demographics: information about a particular population.

Take it further

The Office for National Statistics collects crime statistics for England and Wales. Go to the following release bulletin, 'Crime in England and Wales: Year Ending March 2018' (https://www.ons.gov.uk/peoplepopulationand community/crimeandjustice/bulletins/crimeinenglandand wales/yearendingmarch 2018) and record some statistics for the previous 12 months. Then consider if demographics could provide reasons for the statistics.

This AC has appeared in recent exam question papers.

Sample answers

Answer A

The way society portrays certain behaviour can have a major impact on how this behaviour is dealt with. Society's norms and values can have a huge impact on creating laws, amending laws or abolishing laws through methods such as campaigning or decriminalisation. Homosexuality was illegal before 1967; however, people in society over time changed their attitudes about this subject and became more accepting of it, leading eventually to same-sex marriages.

Also, with smoking the attitudes from society used to be very relaxed and accepting of smoking. However, since medical evidence has shown the links to cancer and other illnesses, the views of society have changed. Laws such as those against smoking inside a public building were introduced in 2007. New laws or new policies have been put in place to tackle crime and make society a safer place. Also, some policies are informal such as community strategies, rather than government laws, will also be shaped by society as they are dependent on society's views.

This answer would receive **5/7**. The answer below shows how it can be improved with the additions in bold.

Answer B

The way society portrays certain behaviour can have a major impact on how this behaviour is dealt with. Society's norms and values can have a huge impact on creating laws, amending laws or abolishing laws through methods such as campaigning or decriminalisation. Homosexuality was illegal before 1967 **when the age of consent for homosexuality was set at 21 years. Eventually, this was lowered to 16 years, by the Sexual Offences (Amendment) Act 2000.** However, people in society over time changed their attitudes about this subject and became more accepting of it, leading eventually to same-sex marriages **in 2014 by the Marriage (Same Sex Couples) Act 2013.**

Exam tip

Always add examples in an exam answer to increase marks. This can include the names of laws or Acts of Parliament to provide detail.

Also, with smoking the attitudes from society used to be very relaxed and accepting of smoking. However, since medical evidence, **particularly the Surgeon General's Report (USA) in 1964**, has shown the links to cancer and other illnesses the views of society have changed. Laws such as those against smoking inside a public building were introduced in 2007 **by the Health Act 2006**. New laws or new policies have been put in place to tackle crime and make society a safer place. **Such laws included the Children and Families Act 2014, which enabled the government to implement regulations to prohibit smoking in vehicles when children are present**. Also, some policies that are informal such as community strategies, rather than government laws, will also be shaped by society as they are dependent on society's views. **This could include the offer of youth groups and community courses to educate people.**

Test yourself

1. How have society's views on smoking changed over time?
2. Give two examples of changes in the law on the smoking of cigarettes.
3. Explain how the law on homosexuality has changed and when this happened.
4. When and why did England and Wales abolish the death penalty?
5. State an Act of Parliament that supports the rights of women.
6. Identify, as a synoptic link, a campaign for change that can be linked to the changing laws on domestic violence.

CHECKLIST – ARE YOU ABLE TO:

☐ explain and give examples of the terms social values, norms and mores

☐ explain a range of areas of policy development linked to changes in society

☐ understand the synoptic links to Unit 1 and the public perception of crime, evaluating methods of collecting statistics about crime and campaigning to change the law or introduce a new policy?

Explore online

Read the article by Olivia Petter (2018, 29 October) 'Upskirting: What is it and Why are People Trying to Make it Illegal?' and watch the short video clip (both at https://www.independent.co.uk/life-style/upskirting-explained-law-rules-criminal-offence-photos-skirt-consent-women-gina-martin-a8401011.html).

Now answer the following questions:
1. How would you define upskirting?
2. How long in prison could people face if they are guilty of upskirting?
3. What is the difference in the law about upskirting between England and Wales, and Scotland?
4. Explain the campaign methods used to promote the campaign.
5. While this proposal was blocked, research the government's current position on this policy.

The government plan is to make upskirting a criminal offence.

Synoptic link

This campaign could also be studied under various ACs in Unit 1 as it is a campaign for change.

AC4.3 DISCUSS HOW CAMPAIGNS AFFECT POLICY MAKING

See pages 137–144 of the textbook.

Synoptic link

This AC is a key synoptic link to Unit 1. Campaigns for change are the focus of Unit 1 and this AC is focused on how campaigns can affect policy development or change the law.

Exam tip ✔

Make sure that in your answer you can include the actual changes in policy or the law that the campaigns have helped introduce.

Activity 2.23

Campaign

Match the campaign to the policy development:

A. Sarah's law ☐

B. The Equal Love campaign and other groups supporting same-gender relationships ☐

C. Bobby Turnbull's campaign ☐

D. Ann Ming's campaign/Stephen Lawrence campaign ☐

E. Lillian's law ☐

F. Claire's law ☐

G. Brexit campaign ☐

H. ASH/British Lung Foundation and other health charities ☐

Policy development

1. Drug Driving (Specified Limits) (England and Wales) Regulations 2014

2. Amendments to the Firearms Act 1968, preventing any person who receives a suspended sentence of three months or more for any offence from purchasing or possessing a firearm

3. Health Act 2006, prohibiting smoking in enclosed and substantially enclosed work and public places

4. European Union Withdrawal Act 2018

5. Marriage (Same Sex Couples) Act 2013 and the legalisation of same-sex marriage

6. Criminal Justice Act 2003 – the abolition of double jeopardy for murder and other serious offences

7. Domestic Abuse Disclosure Scheme

8. Child Sex Offenders Disclosure Scheme

CAMPAIGN

Campaigns help to promote policy development.

Exam tip ✔

You will not be asked to discuss a named campaign but may be asked to discuss:

- individual campaigns and/or
- newspaper campaigns and/or
- pressure group campaigns.

Summary of campaigns and policies

Campaign	Type of campaign	Reason behind campaign	Campaign methods	Policy introduced
Sarah's law  Sarah Payne abducted and killed in 2000.	Newspaper/ individual. The *News of the World* backed the campaign led by Sarah's mother, Sara Payne. Similar to the American campaign called Megan's law.	Abduction and murder of 8-year-old Sarah by Roy Whiting, who was on the Sex Offenders Register for abducting and indecently assaulting a young girl.	A petition promoted by the *News of the World* received 700,000 signatures.	Child Sex Offender Disclosure Scheme. Allows people who are able to protect children to apply for details of those living in the area with convictions for child sex offences. Initially a pilot scheme, it was introduced and extended to all areas in England and Wales in 2011.
Bobby Turnbull's campaign Bobby Turnbull	Individual campaign. Bobby Turnbull started a campaign to change the gun laws when members of his family were shot and killed.	Bobby Turnbull's mother, sister and aunt were killed on New Year's Day 2012 by Michael Atherton. Atherton had a history of domestic violence and his guns had been removed from him at one stage but were later returned.	A petition to change the gun laws gained 20,000 signatures. Bobby Turnbull also regularly appeared in the media and lobbied MPs.	Amendment to the Firearms Act 1968 preventing any person who receives a suspended sentence of three months or more, for any offence, from purchasing or possessing a firearm. Plus every incident of domestic violence promotes a police review of a firearms certificate.

(Continued) »

Campaign	Type of campaign	Reason behind campaign	Campaign methods	Policy introduced
Lillian's law Lillian Groves was killed by a driver who had taken drugs.	Individual campaign. Lead by Lillian's family as there were no specific offences to cover drug driving, unlike drink driving.	Lillian Groves was aged 14 when she was killed by a car driver who had taken cannabis. Lillian's mother and father promoted the campaign to change the laws concerning drug driving.	A petition was signed by more than 22,000 people. Mrs Natasha Groves wrote to every MP encouraging them to back the changes in Parliament. She also appeared with Lillian's aunt on the TV show *This Morning*.	The Drug Driving (Specified Limits) (England and Wales) Regulations 2014 came into force in March 2015. Changes included making drug driving a specific criminal offence and introducing random drug spot checks.

Example questions

Previous exam questions on this AC include:

Unit 2 2017 exam paper E*xplain how campaigns such as reinstating capital punishment might influence policy making. [5 marks]*

Unit 2 2018 exam paper *Discuss campaigns that have resulted in a change in the law. [8 marks]*

Using the mark scheme below, consider how many marks the sample answer to the **Unit 2 2018 exam question** above, shown on the following page, should receive. Then check your view with the online suggested answers.

1–3 marks: Answers that discuss in limited detail campaigns that have resulted in a change in the law. Answers convey meaning but lack detail. Little or no use of specialist vocabulary.

4–6 marks: Answers that discuss in some detail campaigns that have resulted in a change in law. Where only one campaign is discussed in detail the mark is capped at a maximum of 5. Answers communicate meaning with some use of specialist vocabulary.

7–8 marks: Answers that discuss in detail campaigns that have resulted in a change in law. Answers are well structured and clearly expressed. Specialist terms are used with ease and accuracy.

Explore online

Read 'How We Changed the Law on Stalking' (2012, 10 April) by Harry Fletcher and Laura Richards on the *Guardian* website (https://www.theguardian.com/society/2012/apr/10/how-we-changed-stalking-law), then research the campaign to make stalking a criminal offence. Record details similar to those in the table above.

Sample answer

One example of a campaign that has resulted in a change in the law is Sarah's law campaign. Sarah was a young girl who was raped and killed by a known sex offender in the area. Sarah's parents campaigned to bring in a law (similar to Megan's law in the USA) which allowed parents and carers to find out from the police if there were any known sex offenders living in the area. Another campaign that resulted in a change in the law is the double jeopardy law campaign. Julie Hogg was murdered by her former boyfriend (Billy Dunlop) and he was tried and found innocent twice and therefore allowed to go free. However, Julie's parents campaigned for the double jeopardy law to be changed so that if there was new and compelling evidence then a suspect could be tried again. Billy Dunlop was charged and tried and then found guilty of Julie's murder as a result of a change in the law. Another campaign is ASH (anti-smoking campaign), which banned an adult from smoking in a car if a child was present.

Exam tip ✓

When answering a question on this AC, remember to explain who promoted the campaign for change and the campaign methods used. In addition, the actual name of the change, whether it is a law, policy, scheme, etc., should be added. Also try to briefly explain the change introduced.

A recent campaign, which helped to introduce a new government minister, is that started by Matthew Smith, whose brother Dan died by suicide. He joined forces with CALM (Campaign Against Living Miserably) which had started Project 84, so called because 84 men commit suicide every week. Their campaign methods included a petition that gained almost 400,000 signatures. Also, they erected 84 sculptures of men on the roof top of the building used by the TV show *This Morning*. As a result of campaigning, a new minister, Jackie Doyle-Price, was appointed in October 2018. The position being the Minister for Mental Health, Inequalities and Suicide Prevention.

CAMPAIGN AGAINST LIVING MISERABLY CALM

Matthew Smith's campaign helped change the government's policy on suicide prevention.

Test yourself

1. Give an example of an individual campaign for change.
2. Give an example of a newspaper campaign for change.
3. Give an example of a pressure group campaign for change.
4. Which newspaper supported the campaign for Sarah's law?
5. Name the scheme introduced as a result of Sarah's law campaign.
6. Which law did Ann Ming seek to be abolished?
7. Why did Ann Ming start her campaign?
8. Name the law introduced by campaigns such as that of Ann Ming.
9. Why did Bobby Turnbull campaign to change the gun laws?
10. Explain the legal changes introduced as a result of Lillian's law campaign.
11. State two campaigns for change supported by pressure groups.

Ann Ming

CHECKLIST – ARE YOU ABLE TO:

☐ discuss how campaigns affect policy development

☐ consider a range of campaigns by explaining how the law was changed

☐ discuss newspaper campaigns

☐ discuss individual campaigns

☐ discuss pressure group campaigns?

Campaign ideas

If you would like to research some current campaigns go to https://www.change.org/ where you will find many examples for use in your studies.

UNIT 3
CRIME SCENE TO COURTROOM

AC1.1 EVALUATE THE EFFECTIVENESS OF THE ROLES OF PERSONNEL INVOLVED IN CRIMINAL INVESTIGATIONS

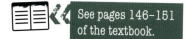

See pages 146–151 of the textbook.

As a minimum, make sure you include four roles with detailed evaluation.

Controlled assessment tip

This AC is worth 10 marks and requires an evaluation of the roles. To access the top mark band, include a clear and detailed evaluation of the effectiveness of each role in criminal investigations. You should include strengths, limitations and case examples to support your evaluation.

Roles of personnel

Activity 3.1

Add strengths and limitations of each role to the mind map on the next page.

Controlled assessment tip

Your evaluation should always focus on how effective these roles are in a criminal investigation. For example, it is not simply the positives of being a pathologist or police officer, but rather how effective (or ineffective) these roles can be during criminal investigations. When focusing on limitations, you should consider cost, expertise and availability.

Need some hints? Refer to pages 146–151 of the textbook.

Scenes of crime officers

Strengths	Limitations

Police officers

Strengths	Limitations

Evaluation of the effectiveness of the roles

Pathologists

Strengths	Limitations

Forensic scientists

Strengths	Limitations

Explore online

Research the following case examples and record research for each case by answering the questions below:

Cases
- Stephen Lawrence 1993
- Hillsborough Football Disaster 1989
- Adam Scott 2011
- Alps Massacre Investigation 2012.

1. Which role of personnel can be evaluated through this case?
2. Was the personnel used effectively or ineffectively in this case? How?

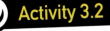

Activity 3.2

Time for improvements

Read the section of AC1.1 below. This is one paragraph, taken from AC1.1, which evaluates the effectiveness of police officers in criminal investigations.

Police officers

Police officers are very important in criminal investigations.

First of all, the starting salery for police officers is between £19,971 and £ 23,000. This provides an insentive for people to join the proffession, this means there will be many officers to help in criminal investigations. Police officers can specialise in the force in units/sections such as firearms or CID (Criminal Investigation Department). This means if you join the police force there are many routes of progression in terms of careers.

However, at times, police officers may make mistakes during criminal investigatons. Sometimes police may be placed under intence pressure to prevent crime or arrest criminals and this may lead to errors in investigations.

Police officers were present during the Gareth Hughes case.

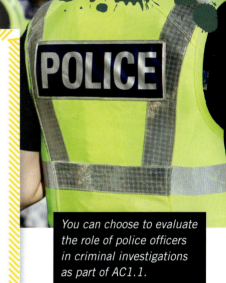

You can choose to evaluate the role of police officers in criminal investigations as part of AC1.1.

Read the assessor commentary below about the quality of this paragraph.

Assessor commentary

- This candidate has selected a relevant role of personnel.
- The strengths are not focused on the effectiveness of police officers in criminal investigations, but rather the positives of joining the police force. This would need amending and developing in order to achieve high marks. The candidate should add more strengths to this paragraph too.
- The limitations are focused on the effectiveness of the police during investigations, however the limitations are too brief. A detailed evaluation would be needed for each role.
- The limitations should consider cost, expertise and availability for each role in order to achieve high marks. This is not considered here.

(Continued)

- No reference is made to an existing case example to support the evaluation, such as Stephen Lawrence or the Hillsborough Disaster, etc.
- It is good to see a link to the assignment brief, however the candidate merely states that police officers were present during the Gareth Hughes case. Here the candidate could evaluate the effectiveness of the roles in Gareth Hughes to support their general evaluative comments. This would be evidence of good practice.

Now it is over to you to improve this paragraph. Correct any literacy errors and use the assessor commentary above to create the perfect paragraph about police officers.

Activity 3.3

How would the points in the Link to brief on this page demonstrate effectiveness or ineffectiveness of the police officers in the Gareth Hughes brief?

CHECKLIST – HAVE YOU INCLUDED:

- [ ] a range of personnel – minimum of four needed
- [ ] a clear and detailed evaluation of the effectiveness of the roles of personnel in criminal investigations; needs to include strengths and limitations
- [ ] limitations that focus on cost, availability and expertise
- [ ] examples (cases to support evaluation)
- [ ] links to the assignment brief where relevant?

Link to brief

Gareth Hughes

Consider the role of the police officers in the case of Gareth Hughes:

- The police, keen to involve the press in catching the killer, allowed a journalist from a local paper access to the area to take photos of the crime scene. Intense pressure was put on the police from the outset to catch the killer.
- To build a case against Hughes, the police deployed a team of officers to befriend him using Facebook. This was in an attempt to make him confess.
- Cross-contamination of evidence, as both items (Hughes' trainers and the red scarf) were stored in the same evidence bag: 'Interviewing officer – I am now putting the items back into the evidence bag.'

AC1.2 ASSESS THE USEFULNESS OF INVESTIGATIVE TECHNIQUES IN CRIMINAL INVESTIGATIONS

See pages 152–160 of the textbook.

Investigative techniques

Activity 3.4

Complete the following four tables for each investigative technique. The cases and links to the assignment brief have been suggested, however these need to be explained in depth. Please remember these cases are simply suggestions and you may wish to use alternative case examples.

These tables could be used to help you structure your information in the controlled assessment for AC1.2; however, remember that your work must be in detailed paragraphs, not written as a table.

Controlled assessment tip

This AC is worth 20 marks, therefore a significant amount of time should be allocated to it during the Unit 3 controlled assessment. It is the AC that carries the most marks.

Key term

Assess: to make a judgement about the quality or value of something. In other words, is the investigative technique useful when investigating crimes and, if so, in which types of criminal investigations?

Investigative technique	Intelligence databases storing forensic evidence (DNA or deoxyribonucleic evidence)
Explanation of technique (very brief)	
Strengths of the technique (how it is useful in criminal investigations)	
Limitations of the technique (how it may not be useful in criminal investigations)	
Which criminal investigations is the technique most useful in and why? For example: situations such as crime scene, laboratory, police station or street. Or types of crime such as: violent, e-crime, property crime, etc.	
Case examples to support assessment	Colin Pitchfork, Colette Aram, David Butler, etc.
Link to assignment brief (only where relevant) **Was the technique used effectively or not?**	Gareth Hughes: cross-contamination of evidence (trainers and scarf) placed in the same bag.

Investigative technique	Surveillance (CCTV, covert human intelligence sources, phone logs, etc.)
Explanation of technique (very brief)	
Strengths of the technique (how it is useful in criminal investigations)	
Limitations of the technique (how it may not be useful in criminal investigations)	
Which criminal investigations is the technique most useful in and why? For example: situations such as crime scene, laboratory, police station or street. Or types of crime such as: violent, e-crime, property crime, etc.	
Case examples to support assessment	London riots, James Bulger, Colin Stagg, etc.
Link to assignment brief (only where relevant) Was the technique used effectively or not?	Gareth Hughes: Facebook used as an attempt to make Hughes confess.

Explore online

The use of CCTV in criminal investigations

Read 'The High Street Abduction' on the BBC News website (https://www.bbc.co.uk/news/resources/idt-5667c315-a69c-4e5d-a683-e4e7771eb04d) to assess the usefulness of CCTV during a high street abduction in Newcastle City Centre 2016.

This could be used as a case example to support your assessment of surveillance.

CCTV can be used as an investigative technique in criminal cases.

Investigative technique	Profiling techniques (typological profiling, investigative psychology and geographical profiling)
Explanation of technique (very brief)	
Strengths of the technique (how it is useful in criminal investigations)	
Limitations of the technique (how it may not be useful in criminal investigations)	

(Continued)

Which criminal investigations is the technique most useful in and why? For example: situations such as crime scene, laboratory, police station or street. Or types of crime such as: violent, e-crime, property crime, etc.	
Case examples to support assessment	John Duffy, Yorkshire Ripper, Colin Stagg, etc.
Link to assignment brief (only where relevant) **Was the technique used effectively or not?**	Gareth Hughes: 'They also enlisted the help of a criminal psychologist to create an offender profile of the killer. This led them to arrest a local man, Gareth Hughes, who matched the offender profile and has previous convictions against women.'

Investigative technique	Interview: • Eye-witness testimony and experts
Explanation of technique (very brief)	
Strengths of the technique (how it is useful in criminal investigations)	
Limitations of the technique (how it may not be useful in criminal investigations)	

(Continued)

Which criminal investigations is the technique most useful in and why? For example: situations such as crime scene, laboratory, police station or street. Or types of crime such as: violent, e-crime, property crime, etc.	
Case examples to support assessment	Eye witness: Ronald Cotton Experts: Leanne Tiernan, Alice Ruggles, etc.
Link to assignment brief (only where relevant) **Was the technique used effectively or not?**	Gareth Hughes: 'A witness also came forward whilst the police were in the park. He told officers there that he had seen a man acting suspiciously, earlier in the evening near the park.' 'Following a Crime Watch appeal two weeks after the murder, a second eye witness came forward. This person claimed to have seen a man acting suspiciously on the night in question.'

Need some hints? Refer to pages 152–160 of the textbook.

Controlled assessment tip

Your assessment of the techniques must be clear and detailed in order to access the top mark band. Please remember that when it comes to including case examples to support your assessment, you should not simply be describing the cases, but rather focusing on how the technique was used in that case. Was it used effectively or ineffectively?

Eye witnesses may be asked to provide evidence in court.

CHECKLIST – HAVE YOU INCLUDED:

☐ a wide range of investigative techniques (the tables on pages 101–104 are divided into four main areas; however, all four areas include additional techniques, as in line with the specification)

☐ a clear and detailed assessment of the usefulness of the investigative techniques in criminal investigations

☐ examples (cases to support the assessment)

☐ links to the assignment brief where relevant?

AC1.3 EXPLAIN HOW EVIDENCE IS PROCESSED

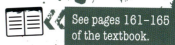

See pages 161-165 of the textbook.

Types of evidence

Physical evidence	Testimonial evidence
Physical evidence refers to real evidence. This may consist of tangible articles such as hairs, fibres and fingerprints or biological material such as blood.	Testimonial evidence refers to statements or the spoken word from the defendant (the suspect), a victim or witnesses.

Blood may be found at crime scenes and would be regarded as physical evidence. It would be collected and may be used as evidence during a criminal trial.

Physical evidence

Activity 3.5

Following you will see four diagrams with different types of evidence in the centre. Surrounding each type of evidence are important terms/phrases that relate to the collection, transfer, storage and analysis of that type of evidence.

Use the important terms to create four paragraphs explaining how the physical evidence is processed in a criminal investigation. Please feel free to add more terms based on your own knowledge/research.

Controlled assessment tip

The focus of AC1.3 is how the evidence is processed. It requires a clear and detailed explanation of how evidence is processed, this includes the collection, transfer, storage and analysis of evidence. You must also consider the personnel involved, for example consider how evidence may be collected by scene of crime officers and analysed by forensic scientists/specialists.

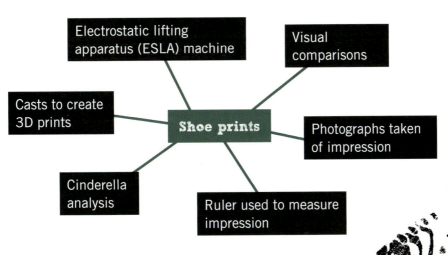

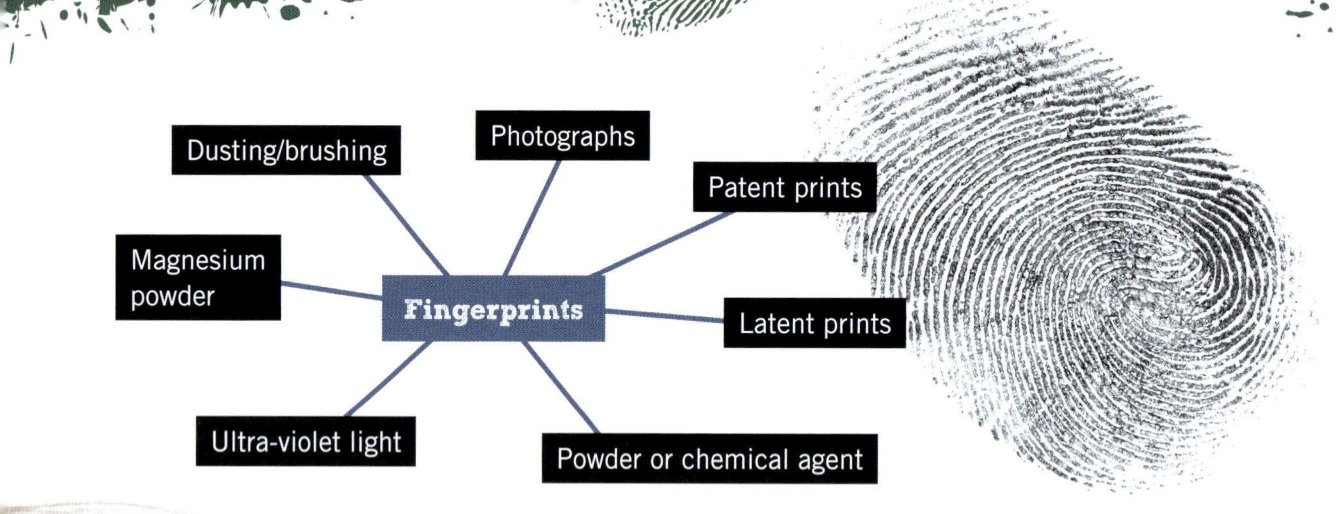

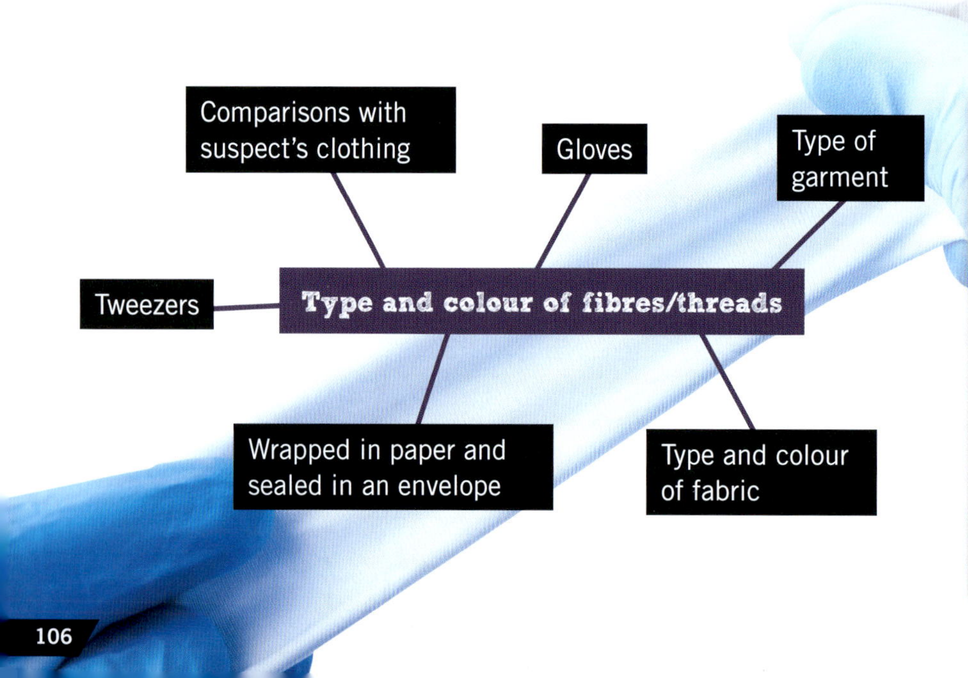

Dusting/brushing

Photographs

Patent prints

Magnesium powder

Fingerprints

Latent prints

Ultra-violet light

Powder or chemical agent

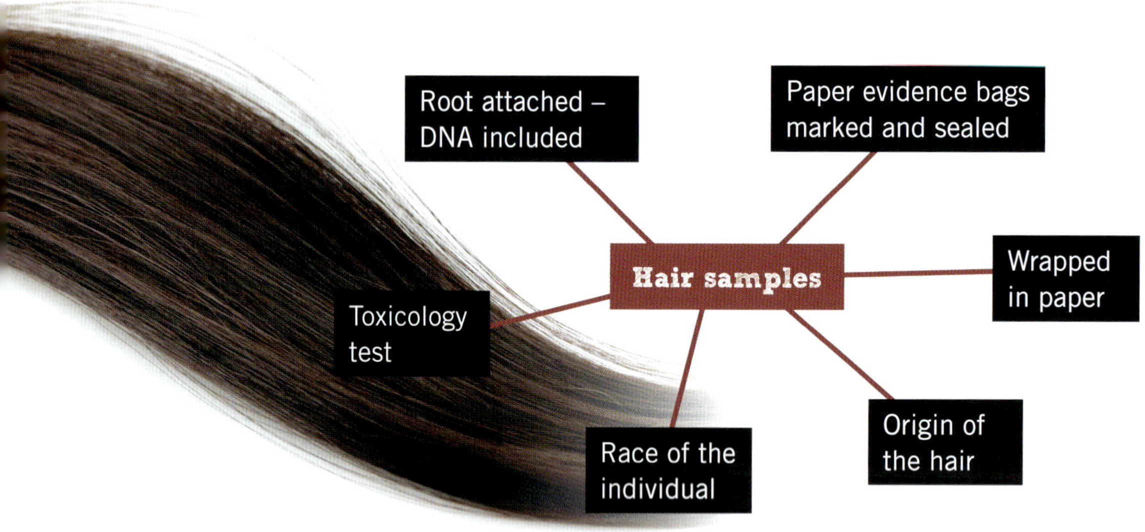

Root attached – DNA included

Paper evidence bags marked and sealed

Hair samples

Wrapped in paper

Toxicology test

Origin of the hair

Race of the individual

Comparisons with suspect's clothing

Gloves

Type of garment

Tweezers

Type and colour of fibres/threads

Wrapped in paper and sealed in an envelope

Type and colour of fabric

Controlled assessment tip

In the controlled assessment, explain physical and testimonial evidence. Then select the relevant examples of physical evidence from the assignment brief to explain these relevant examples of evidence in detail, focusing on the process of evidence.

Testimonial evidence

Testimonial evidence refers to statements or the spoken word from the defendant (the suspect), a victim or witnesses.

Testimonial evidence must be admissible, which means it complies with the rules of evidence in the courtroom. In the Colin Stagg case, the evidence relating to 'Lizzie' was excluded.

Statements of witnesses will be collected before the criminal trial and disclosed prior to the court case. In court, testimonial evidence is given in the witness box. Both the prosecution teams and defence will have the opportunity to question witnesses. On occasion, witness statements can simply be read out at court, without the need for the witness to attend.

Vulnerable witnesses, such as children, can provide evidence via a video link.

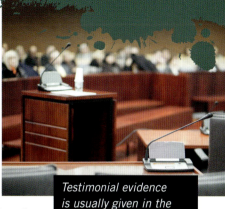

Testimonial evidence is usually given in the witness box in court.

Explore online

Research the three cases below and answer the following questions for each case. This can be added to AC1.3 as your case examples.

Cases: Barry George, Amanda Knox and Sally Clark
1. Briefly outline the facts of the case.
2. Explain how the evidence was used in the case and what type of evidence was involved (physical items such as blood, footprints, etc., or testimonial evidence such as witnesses).
3. Explain whether there are any concerns with the evidence used in this case and why.

Controlled assessment tip

To achieve high marks, you will need to include case examples explaining the evidence used and the issues surrounding it. Do not forget to include this.

Link to brief

In pairs, identify the types of physical evidence found in the assignment brief. Also explain how testimonial evidence will be used in the assignment brief.

CHECKLIST – HAVE YOU INCLUDED:

☐ physical and testimonial evidence

☐ a clear and detailed explanation of how evidence is processed – select relevant types of physical evidence that can be found in the assignment brief

☐ examples (cases to show how evidence is processed)

☐ links to the assignment brief where relevant?

AC1.4 EXAMINE THE RIGHTS OF INDIVIDUALS IN CRIMINAL INVESTIGATIONS

See pages 166–168 of the textbook.

The rights of a suspect

The rights of a suspect include:

- Police can arrest without a warrant if they have reasonable grounds to believe that a person is committing, has committed or is about to commit an offence.
- The arrest must be necessary.
- The suspect must be informed of the arrest and the reason why (S24 Police and Criminal Evidence Act 1984 as amended by the Serious Organised Crime and Police Act 2005).
- The police must caution the suspect, this includes the right to silence.
- The custody officer is responsible for ensuring all rights are followed when the suspect is detained.
- The custody officer reviews the length of detention.
- A suspect must be released within 24 hours of their arrival at the police station. However, this can be extended to 36 hours with permission from the superintendent or up to 96 hours with a magistrate's approval.

When detained, key rights include:

- S56 PACE 1984 – right to inform someone of their arrest.
- S58 PACE 1984 – right to consult privately with a solicitor.
- A right to consult the Codes of Practice.
- Fingerprints and evidence from a mouth swab (DNA) can be taken with reasonable force, without consent.
- Interviews should be tape recorded (or video recorded).
- Suspects are entitled to legal advice during an interview, with the presence of a solicitor.
- 'No comment' interviews are allowed.

During or after trial:

- All suspects are entitled to a fair trial, Article 6 of the Human Rights Act 1998.
- Suspects have the right to appeal against the conviction and/or the sentence.

Controlled assessment tip

To achieve top marks in AC1.4 you need to include the rights of suspects, victims and witnesses.

There are many rights for individuals during criminal investigations, particularly suspects. These rights will apply from the initial arrest.

Appeal routes

Activity 3.6

In pairs, use the flowcharts below to explain the various appeal routes available to the suspect (also known as the defendant).

- The first appeal route is in cases where the trial was heard at a Magistrates' Court.
- The second appeal route is in cases where the trial was heard at a Crown Court.

Add explanations to these flowcharts.

Trial heard at Magistrates' Court

Supreme Court
▲
Court of Appeal
▲
Crown Court
▲
Magistrates' Court

Trial heard at Crown Court

Supreme Court
▲
Court of Appeal
▲
Crown Court

City of London Magistrates' Court

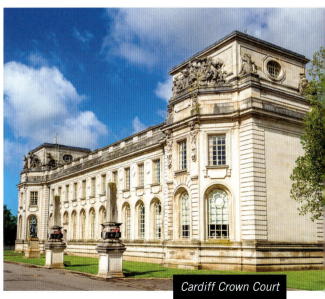

Cardiff Crown Court

The rights of victims and witnesses

The rights of victims	Code of Practice for Victims of Crime – established by the Domestic Violence, Crime and Victims Act 2004: • The right to be kept informed of the progress of the case. • To be informed when a suspect is arrested, charged, bailed or sentenced. • The right to additional help when giving evidence in court if you are vulnerable, intimidated, a child or young person (special measures). • The right to apply for compensation. • The right to make a victim personal statement to explain the impact of the crime.
The rights of witnesses	Witness Charter: • The right to have a main point of contact for information about the case. • The right to claim expenses for travel and loss of earnings incurred during the trial. • The right to receive special measures if you are a vulnerable or intimidated witness. This may include giving evidence by video link, etc.

Link to brief

Refer to the assignment brief and identify any rights of the suspect that have been breached during this case.

CHECKLIST – HAVE YOU INCLUDED:

☐ the rights of the suspect, victims and witnesses

☐ a clear examination of the rights of all individuals in criminal investigations

☐ links to the assignment brief where relevant?

Victims are kept informed from the point of charge through to the conclusion of a case.

LEARNING OUTCOME 2 UNDERSTAND THE PROCESS FOR PROSECUTION OF SUSPECTS

AC2.1 EXPLAIN THE REQUIREMENTS OF THE CROWN PROSECUTION SERVICE (CPS) FOR PROSECUTING SUSPECTS

See pages 169–172 of the textbook.

Explore online

What is the role of the CPS in criminal cases?

Read about the CPS on its website (https://www.cps.gov.uk) to help you explain the role of the CPS in criminal cases.

Consider the following:
- Who works for the CPS?
- What does the CPS do?

Take it further

Watch 'What the CPS Does, and What Happens at Court' on YouTube (https://www.youtube.com/watch?v=i5zn2cbIai8) to find more detailed information about the role of the CPS in criminal cases and the court process.

Mark band 2 specifically asks for clear and relevant examples; therefore, make sure the CPS tests are detailed and include key considerations under each test. It is also advisable to include case examples here to support the explanation, this will help you achieve 4 marks.

Controlled assessment tip

This AC is worth 4 marks and requires a detailed explanation of the requirements of the CPS in prosecuting suspects. You should start the AC by briefly introducing the role of the CPS in criminal trials. You will then need to explain the requirements for prosecuting suspects, this refers to the CPS tests and needs to be detailed.

The CPS website includes key information regarding its role in prosecuting suspects.

Activity 3.7

Read the response on the following page for AC2.1 followed by the assessor commentary.

Create a list of improvements that would be needed in order for this response to gain 4 marks. What could be added to this answer? Correct any literacy errors in the response.

The CPS (Crown Prosecution Service) was established in 1986 in order to create an independant body. Prior to this date, the police would arrest, investigate and procecute suspects. The CPS was established by the Prosecution of offences act 1985.

The role of the CPS is to provide advice to the police officers investigating a case, make a decision regarding the cases that require prosecution and decide the correct charge. Crown prosecutors also prepare cases for court and present the cases in court. Crown Prosecutors may also be barristers and solicitors.

The CPS need to use two tests when deciding whether to prosecute a suspect; the evidential test and the public interest test.

Assessor commentary

The response has started with a brief overview of the role of the CPS and includes reference to legislation that established it.

However, the response fails to explain the requirements for prosecuting suspects in detail, it simply names two tests: the evidential and public interest tests. There is no explanation of the issues or questions considered under each test and the threshold test is also omitted from the answer.

There are no case examples and no reference to the assignment brief.

This answer would be limited to mark band 1 (1–2 marks).

Link to brief

Do you agree with the decision to prosecute made by the CPS in the assignment brief? If so, why?

Consider the following:

Evidential test: the following evidence was found in the Gareth Hughes case: eye witness testimony, DNA on the scarf, footprint evidence, an offender profile and the 'no comment' interview.

Public interest test: the Hughes case involved a murder of a young female suspect. The murder involved a frenzied knife attack in a park.

CHECKLIST – HAVE YOU INCLUDED:

- [ ] a brief introduction covering the role of the CPS
- [ ] a detailed explanation of the requirements of the CPS in prosecuting suspects – all tests that are detailed
- [ ] case examples (to support explanation)
- [ ] links to the assignment brief where relevant?

AC2.2 DESCRIBE TRIAL PROCESSES

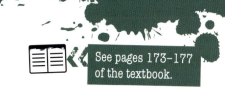
See pages 173–177 of the textbook.

Types of criminal offences

Summary offences	Triable either-way offences	Indictable offences
The least serious offences, including minor offences such as assault and battery. These offences are tried in the Magistrates' Court.	These offences are tried in either the Magistrates' Court or the Crown Court. Examples of either-way offences include theft and burglary.	The most serious offences, including offences such as murder, rape and manslaughter. These offences are tried in the Crown Court.

Criminal courts

 **Activity 3.8**

Complete the table below to explain the various criminal courts in England and Wales.

Include:

- the personnel found in each court
- sentencing powers of the court
- general processes of the court.

Magistrates' Court	Crown Court	Court of Appeal (Criminal Division)	Supreme Court

Bail can be granted by the police or the courts.

Bail

Summary of bail processes

- Bail means the person is allowed to remain at liberty until the next stage in the case. Bail can be granted at any point after the arrest.
- Bail can be granted by the police or the courts.
- Bail can be unconditional with no conditions attached. Or it may be conditional bail. Conditions may include curfew, reporting or residence, etc.
- The reason for imposing conditions would be to ensure that the person: surrenders to bail; does not commit an offence while on bail; and does not interfere with witnesses.
- The power to grant bail from the Magistrates' Court is contained in the Bail Act 1976.
- The Bail Act 1976, Section 4, gives a general right to bail, as there is the assumption that a person is innocent until proven guilty. The Magistrates' Court can refuse to grant bail if there are substantial grounds for believing that if bail were granted the person would: fail to surrender to bail; commit an offence when on bail; interfere with witnesses; or obstruct the course of justice.
- The courts can also refuse bail for the person's own protection.
- The factors that are considered when deciding to grant bail include: the nature and seriousness of the offence; the character, antecedents, associations and community ties of the defendant; the defendant's record of previous bail; and the strength of the evidence.

Plea bargaining

Plea bargaining is an arrangement agreed by the prosecution and defence, or the judge, as an incentive for the defendant to plead guilty. It could concern the charge or the sentence. For example, the defendant may agree to plead guilty to a lesser charge (manslaughter instead of murder) or the defendant may be told in advance what their sentence will be if they plead guilty.

Link to brief

The assignment brief of Gareth Hughes states the following:

Hughes was kept in custody for three days, where he asserted that he was abroad at the time of the murder; he refused to give any other comments during interview. With no forensic evidence linking him to the crime, he was released on bail.

1. Why was Hughes granted bail originally?
2. Do you agree with this decision to grant bail?

The assignment brief continues to state the following:

Several months later Hughes was re-arrested and re-interviewed.

On the advice of the Crown Prosecution Service the police charged Hughes with murder. He was remanded in custody.

3. Why was Hughes not granted bail in this second instance?
4. Do you agree with this decision to refuse bail?

Appeals

The appeal routes are as follows:

Trial heard at Magistrates' Court

Supreme Court
▲
Court of Appeal
▲
Crown Court
▲
Magistrates' Court

Trial heard at Crown Court

Supreme Court
▲
Court of Appeal
▲
Crown Court

Controlled assessment tip

It is important to cover each stage of the trial process here, including the roles of the personnel involved. However, consider time management when addressing this AC. The stages of the trial process need to be described in some detail, although it is only worth 4 marks.

CHECKLIST – HAVE YOU INCLUDED:

☐ the stages of the trial process in some detail

☐ the personnel involved in the trial process

☐ links to the assignment brief where relevant?

AC2.3 UNDERSTAND RULES IN RELATION TO THE USE OF EVIDENCE IN CRIMINAL CASES

 See pages 178–181 of the textbook.

The use of evidence in court

🔍 **Activity 3.9** //

The diagram below includes key rules of evidence relevant to this AC. Copy it and do the following:

1. Add detailed explanations of these rules to the diagram.
2. Add the legislation listed to the appropriate rule of evidence.

- Criminal Justice Act 2003
- S78 Police & Criminal Evidence Act 1984 (PACE 1984)
- S103 Criminal Justice Act 2003
- Criminal Procedure and Investigations Act 1996
- Article 6 European Convention on Human Rights
- Criminal Justice & Public Order Act 1994
- S114 (1) Criminal Justice Act 2003.

Controlled assessment tip

This AC focuses on how evidence can be used in court. The focus is on the rules of evidence such as relevance and admissibility, disclosure, hearsay and exceptions, and legislation and case law. A detailed understanding of the rules in relation to the use of evidence is needed to gain 4 marks; however, do remember that you are a Criminology student and not necessarily a Law student. Be careful with time management as the AC is worth 4 marks.

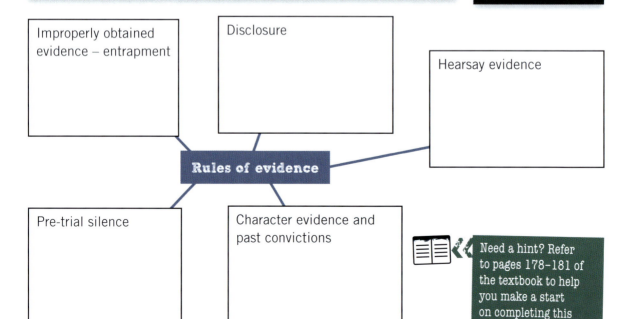

Improperly obtained evidence – entrapment

Disclosure

Hearsay evidence

Rules of evidence

Pre-trial silence

Character evidence and past convictions

📖 Need a hint? Refer to pages 178–181 of the textbook to help you make a start on completing this diagram.

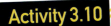

Activity 3.10

Which rules of evidence do the following cases concern and why?

• Colin Stagg
• Sally Clark

Add these two cases to your diagram on the previous page.

CHECKLIST – HAVE YOU INCLUDED:

☐ the rules in relation to the use of evidence in criminal cases
☐ reference to legislation or case law/case examples
☐ links to the assignment brief where relevant?

Link to brief

In the assignment brief (Gareth Hughes) the following evidence may be in question:

• the Facebook operation
• the 'no comment' interview – 'Hughes asserted that he was abroad at the time of the murder; he refused to give any other comments during interview.'
• Appendix 2 – the list of previous convictions.

Should this evidence be admissible? Justify your response.

Evidence may be regarded as admissible or inadmissible in a courtroom as specific rules can be applied.

AC2.4 ASSESS KEY INFLUENCES AFFECTING THE OUTCOMES OF CRIMINAL CASES

See pages 182–186 of the textbook.

See pages 182–186 of the textbook.

Explore online

Research the case of Oscar Pistorius 2013.

You may also want to watch the two following videos on YouTube:
- 'Oscar Pistorius Trial: The Ballistics Evidence' (https://www.youtube.com/watch?v=8NrfoR9sMu)
- '"Blade Runner" Oscar Pistorius' Prison Sentence More than Doubles After Appeal' (https://www.youtube.com/watch?v=p4-9aWK5MNI).

Consider the following two questions:
1. Were there any key influences during this trial? (Evidence/media, etc.)
2. Explain how these key influences would affect the outcome of the trial. Do you think these influences contributed towards the conviction?

Controlled assessment tip

This AC is worth 10 marks, therefore more time should be allocated to this AC compared with the smaller ones. The focus is to assess the key influences affecting the outcomes of criminal cases. A clear and detailed understanding of the impact will be required to gain high marks. This AC is not simply a description of the influences and descriptions alone will limit an answer to mark band 1.

Oscar Pistorius leaving court in 2014.

How do key influences affect the outcomes of criminal cases?

Five key influences have been selected for the table on the following page from the specification list of influences. The summary table only focuses on the impact of these key influences and will refer to case examples that could be used to support the assessment of how they affect the outcomes of criminal cases.

Please remember these case examples are merely suggestions and alternatives/additional case examples may be used.

Key influence	Impact	Case examples
Media	• No presumption of innocence as the jury may be influenced by the media coverage. • Presumption of guilt, rather than a presumption of innocence, as the public/jury may believe what is printed in the media. • Jury can use evidence from outside the courtroom/outside factors to influence their judgement – this would be regarded as inadmissible evidence. However, it is likely the jury have read/viewed the media coverage, which will influence their decision. • Can affect fairness, as the jury members may be prejudiced. • The jury may be impartial. • Trial by media, rather than trial by jury. This may lead to an unfair trial and breach Article 6 of the European Convention on Human Rights (right to a fair trial).	• Christopher Jefferies • Colin Stagg
Experts	• Expert evidence/testimony can be very influential/persuasive in court. • The jury may lack awareness/understanding of expert statistical evidence, therefore do not doubt its validity/accuracy. • The jury could favour expert evidence and experts (based on statistics/scientific evidence) and be more likely to return a guilty verdict. • There is an assumption that experts and statistics are accurate. • Often the jury is impressed by the expert evidence given. • May lead to a miscarriage of justice.	• Sally Clark • Angela Cannings
Judiciary	• A judge may influence a jury. If the judge appears to be biased or favours one side, the jury may be inclined to follow this opinion. The judge is an experienced legal professional with an understanding of the law, therefore the jury may be persuaded by this rather than considering the facts. • A judge may also hear a case without a jury if the case is too long/complex or there is a fear that jury tampering could occur. This removes the impartiality of a jury of 12 people.	• *R* v *Ponting* • *R* v *Wang* • Twomey 2009

(Continued)

Key influence	Impact	Case examples
Witnesses	• Witnesses could be preferred by jury members as their evidence may be convincing/realistic and believable. This could influence the jury to place a significant amount of weight on that witness and favour either the prosecution or defence, whichever side the witness represents. • However, some witnesses may be unreliable or not credible and therefore their evidence could raise doubts and adversely affect the outcome of a case. Again, this could result in an unfair trial, which may be unjust.	• Damilola Taylor – witness credibility
Politics	• Politics can influence the outcome of criminal cases significantly. • Politics will influence the laws that legislatures enact. For example, if the political focus is to get tough on crime, then laws increasing sentencing can be passed. Likewise, if the political agenda is to deter identified crimes, then harsher sentencing guidelines may be introduced to discourage future crimes. This will affect the outcome of criminal cases, as defendants may be subject to harsher sentencing guidelines than previous cases. • Likewise, politics may affect laws governing individual rights, meaning that in criminal cases the rights of the defendant may be limited as in terrorism cases. This affects the outcomes of criminal cases, as individuals may be treated differently based on the nature of the crime.	• London riots 2011 • Bail • Terrorism offences

The London riots

Remember that in the controlled assessment you must write AC2.4 out in detailed paragraphs. Avoid tables and bullet points as you may sacrifice detail.

In order to access mark band 3 (8–10 marks) make sure you cover a range of key influences (four or five). However do make sure the assessment of their impact in a criminal case is detailed.

Use case examples to support your assessment, focus on how the influence affected the outcome in that particular case.

Link to brief

Gareth Hughes
- How would the media reporting in the case of Gareth Hughes affect the outcome of his case?
- How would the eye witness testimony in the case of Gareth Hughes affect the outcome of his case?

Activity 3.11

1. Select one of the key influences from the table on pages 119–120, and write a detailed paragraph assessing the impact this influence would have on the outcome of a criminal case. Try to include a case example (or two) and make reference to the assignment brief (only if relevant).
2. In pairs, swap paragraphs and peer assess your partner's paragraph.
3. Write down the strengths of your partner's answer and areas for improvement.

CHECKLIST – HAVE YOU INCLUDED:

☐ a clear and detailed assessment of the key influences affecting the outcomes of criminal cases

☐ case examples to support the assessment

☐ links to the assignment brief where relevant?

AC2.5 DISCUSS THE USE OF LAY PEOPLE IN CRIMINAL CASES

See pages 187–191 in the textbook.

Activity 3.12

Working in pairs, assign each person to either the role of a juror or a magistrate.

Your task is to briefly explain your role in a criminal case. Address the following:

1. Who are you?
2. How have you been selected?
3. Which court would you attend?
4. Which criminal cases would you be expected to deal with?
5. What is your role in a criminal case?

Controlled assessment tip

This AC is worth 6 marks; however, remember that the focus is to discuss the strengths and weaknesses of both juries and magistrates in criminal cases.

A jury trial consists of 12 jurors.

Time to evaluate juries and magistrates

Activity 3.13

Read the tables of strengths and weaknesses on the following page for both juries and magistrates. Your task is to develop these tables by adding more strengths and weaknesses.

Juries

Strengths	Weaknesses
• Jury equity – juries are made up of ordinary members of the public who can bring their own 'justice' to a case. Often, juries are more concerned with fairness or morality rather than complex legal principles. • The public have confidence in the jury system as it enables them to participate in a significant role in the Criminal Justice System. • It enables defendants to be tried by their peers and this is viewed as a democratic right.	• The jury may include members who bring prejudice or bias into the decision, this includes racial bias. • Some trials may be too complex for the jury, limiting their understanding of the case and evidence presented. This may be the case for trials involving fraud. • Jurors may be subject to jury tampering or jury nobbling. Jurors may be bribed or intimidated to reach a desired verdict.

Magistrates

Strengths	Weaknesses
• Magistrates are volunteers and therefore only receive expenses. This minimises costs for the Criminal Justice System. • Magistrates will have local knowledge and awareness of community needs, which can be applied to cases. • As magistrates sit in threes, a balanced view is likely to be reached. Also, if all three fail to agree then the majority view will prevail, ensuring fairness.	• Magistrates have received criticism for a lack of diversity on the benches. Magistrates do not adequately represent a cross-section of society as the majority tend to be middle-class and middle-aged, often from professional or managerial roles. • Magistrates have been accused of being prosecution-biased with a tendency to believe police evidence. • Magistrates are not legally trained and may rely heavily on the legal clerk.

Remember, write your discussion of the strengths and weaknesses in paragraphs in the controlled assessment.

Explore online

Research the following cases and add them to the appropriate column of your juries table on page 123.

Consider: does the case illustrate a strength or weakness of juries? If so explain how.
- *R v Owen*
- *R v Ponting*
- *R v Young*
- *R v Kronlid and Others*
- Theodora Dallas
- Joanne Fraill.

Link to brief

Gareth Hughes
- A note was passed from a juror to the trial judge stating that another member of the jury was researching the defendant.
- How would this affect the trial of Gareth Hughes?

CHECKLIST – HAVE YOU INCLUDED:

- [ ] a detailed discussion of the strengths and weaknesses of lay people (juries and magistrates) in criminal cases
- [ ] case examples to support the discussion where relevant
- [ ] links to the assignment brief where relevant?

AC3.1 EXAMINE INFORMATION FOR VALIDITY

See pages 192–197 of the textbook.

Verdicts and judgments

Jeremy Bamber

Jeremy Bamber was convicted of killing five members of his family in 1985 at White House Farm in Essex.

Explore online

Research the case of Jeremy Bamber. The following articles may be useful:
- J B Campaign Ltd (http://www.jeremy-bamber.co.uk).
- 'Scientist's Report Casts Doubt on Jeremy Bamber Trial Evidence', Eric Allison and Simon Hattenstone (2018, 21 September), the *Guardian* (https://www.theguardian.com/uk-news/2018/sep/21/scientists-report-casts-doubt-on-jeremy-bamber-trial-evidence).
- 'Jeremy Bamber Still Waits for the Evidence that Might Clear His Name', Simon Hattenstone and Eric Allison (2017, 24 March), the *Guardian* (https://www.theguardian.com/commentisfree/2017/mar/24/jeremy-bamber-waits-evidence-clear-name-essex-police).

Create a table including the evidence or case facts that appear to be valid and those which appear to lack validity.

Validity	Lack of validity

Now it is time to reach a judgement. Do you think the judgment made in the Jeremy Bamber case is valid or not? Your answer should be justified with key points from your table.

Key terms

Examine: inspect, scrutinise or observe.

Validity: does it have authority, weight, strength or soundness? In other words, it is accurate? For example, ask if a verdict from a criminal case is a valid decision or not?

Controlled assessment tip

This AC is worth 15 marks and requires you to examine a relevant range of information sources. After this examination, you should be able to include a clear and detailed review of their suitability in terms of validity. You need to appreciate that not everything is valid or accurate. Some information sources may lack validity or may include bias. Some sources may include subjective opinion or may be outdated.

After examining each information source, you should reach a judgement regarding the validity of that source or the content of that source.

Activity 3.14

Research the case of Siôn Jenkins, convicted and then later released for the murder of Billie-Jo Jenkins in 1997.
1. Is this judgment valid? Justify your answer.

Evidence

Sir Roy Meadow provided expert evidence concerning the likelihood and causes of sudden infant death syndrome (SIDS) in the cases of Sally Clark and Angela Cannings. Both women were convicted of the murder of their children and later released.

Activity 3.15

In pairs, research and examine the expert evidence provided by Sir Roy Meadow in the cases of Sally Clark and Angela Cannings.
1. Was this expert evidence valid? Justify your response.

Media reports

Media and news reports should remain objective and impartial so as to produce validity. However, at times, reporting may have compromised impartiality or gone so far as to include subjective opinion or political bias.

Explore online

Use the following links and your own additional research to hold a debate in small groups.

One group will put forward an argument to support the validity of media reports, while the other group will put forward an argument claiming that media reporting lacks validity and includes bias or opinion.

Look at the following articles to help you form your argument:
- 'BBC Accused of Political Bias – on the Right, Not the Left', Ian Burrell (2014, 14 February), the *Independent* (https://www.independent.co.uk/news/uk/politics/bbc-accused-of-political-bias-on-the-right-not-the-left-9129639.html).
- 'BBC Accused of Brexit Bias by More than 70 MPs in Open Letter', Ashley Cowburn (2017, 21 March), the *Independent* (https://www.independent.co.uk/news/uk/politics/over-70-mps-write-open-letter-to-bbc-accusing-broadcaster-of-bias-a7640756.html).
- 'BBC Rated Most Accurate and Reliable TV News, Says Ofcom Poll', Jasper Jackson (2015, 16 December), BBC News (https://www.theguardian.com/media/2015/dec/16/bbc-rated-most-accurate-and-reliable-tv-news-says-ofcom-poll).

Media reports should remain objective and impartial.

A judgment from an official inquiry

The Hillsborough disaster

On 15 April 1989, at the start of the FA cup semi-final football match between Liverpool and Nottingham Forest at Sheffield Wednesday's Hillsborough stadium, a panic led to a crush in the steel terraces, leading to the death of 96 Liverpool fans and injuring hundreds more.

Flowers to commemorate the 96 fans who died during the Hillsborough football disaster in 1989.

Explore online

Read the following articles and do your own research to examine the validity of the original Hillsborough Inquiry. Was it valid or not? Justify your answer.

- 'The Long Road to Justice: Hillsborough Disaster Timeline', David Conn (2017, 28 June), the *Guardian* (https://www.theguardian.com/football/2017/jun/28/long-road-justice-hillsborough-inquest-timeline).
- 'Hillsborough Inquests: What You Need to Know' (2016, 26 April), BBC News (https://www.bbc.co.uk/news/uk-england-merseyside- 35383110).
- 'Hillsborough Disaster: CPS Will Not Charge Five Police Officers Over Deaths of 96 Liverpool Fans', Lizzie Dearden (2018, 14 March), the *Independent* (https://www.independent.co.uk/news/uk/crime/hillsborough-disaster-cps-liverpool-police-officers-fan-deaths-prosecutions-david-duckenfield-a8255081.html).

Controlled assessment tip

Remember, your examination must be detailed, with a clear review in terms of validity in order to access the top mark band and achieve 11–15 marks.

CHECKLIST – HAVE YOU INCLUDED:

- ☐ a detailed examination of a range of information sources
- ☐ a clear review of the suitability of the information sources in terms of validity
- ☐ case examples to support the examination and review
- ☐ links to the assignment brief where relevant?

AC3.2 DRAW CONCLUSIONS FROM INFORMATION

See pages 198–202 of the book.

Remember, you should be drawing objective conclusions on the assignment brief here. However, you MUST also consider additional criminal cases. After all, it is a 15 mark AC.

Conclusions

With approximately 130,000 criminal cases every year appearing before the Crown Courts, it is no surprise that the vast majority of cases will result in a just and safe verdict. Most cases include a verdict that is deemed as just, where the law has been applied appropriately and, based on the evidence, the verdict is one of fairness.

However, there have been instances where justice is not achieved, resulting in cases that can be regarded as a miscarriage of justice.

For this AC, you should draw objective conclusions about the Criminal Justice System in England and Wales by analysing information from criminal cases.

Miscarriage of justice

Activity 3.16

Select **three** cases from the list of cases below. These cases could all be regarded as miscarriages of justice.

Your task is to conduct individual research into these cases and answer the following questions for each case:

1. What happened in this case?

2. Why was this case considered to be a miscarriage of justice? Include evidence to support your reasoning.

3. Draw objective conclusions from this criminal case. Include evidence to support your conclusions. For example, does the Criminal Justice System take a considerable amount of time to achieve justice? Does the Criminal Justice System adequately protect the rights of defendants or suspects?

Cases:
- Derek Bentley
- Stefan Kiszko
- Timothy Evans
- Stephen Downing
- Sean Hodgson
- the Birmingham Six
- Sally Clark
- the Guildford Four.

Alternative criminal cases can be used.

> **Controlled assessment tip**
>
> This AC is worth 15 marks and you need to draw objective conclusions on criminal cases, using evidence and clear reasoning in support of these conclusions.

> **Key term**
>
> **Miscarriage of justice:** a criminal case where the defendant has been convicted for a crime which he/she did not commit. It is the conviction of an innocent person.

> *A miscarriage of justice involves the conviction of a person for a crime that they did not commit.*

Just verdicts

Stephen Lawrence

The case of Stephen Lawrence took over 18 years to secure justice.

Need a hint? Refer to page 199 of the textbook.

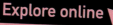

Explore online

Using your own independent research and the web links below, answer the following questions:
- 'Stephen Lawrence Murder: A Timeline of How the Story Unfolded' (2018, 13 April), BBC News (https://www.bbc.co.uk/news/uk-26465916).
- 'Stephen Lawrence 25 Years on: What Happened and Was this Really a Murder that Changed a Nation?', Adam Luscher (2018, 15 April), the *Independent* (https://www.independent.co.uk/news/uk/home-news/stephen-lawrence-murder-25-years-changed-a-nation-police-institutional-racism-macpherson-anniversary-a8307871.html).
1. What happened in the case of Stephen Lawrence (1993)?
2. Was a just verdict eventually achieved? If so, when? If so, who and what contributed to this successful prosecution?
3. What conclusions can be drawn regarding the police investigation? Include evidence to support your conclusions.

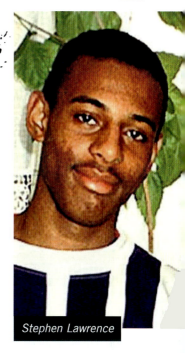

Stephen Lawrence

Just sentencing

In the vast majority of criminal cases, the sentence the defendant receives is just.

However, just like an unjust or unsafe verdict, at times sentencing can be criticised when it appears to be unduly lenient or unfair. If a sentence is regarded as unduly lenient, it can be reviewed as part of the Unduly Lenient Sentence Scheme, after which sentences can be increased.

Examples of unduly lenient sentences include:

- Ian Paterson 2017: a surgeon who performed unnecessary breast operations had his sentence increased from 15 to 20 years.
- Stuart Hall: a BBC presenter had his sentence doubled for sexual assaults from 15 months to 30 months in 2013.
- Rhys Hobbs: a defendant who killed his former girlfriend had his custodial sentence increased from 8 to 12½ years in 2016.

Stuart Hall had his sexual assault sentence doubled.

Explore online

Read the following article and answer the questions below:

'Scores of Prison Sentences Declared "Unduly Lenient" After Victims Complain', Fiona Keating (2017, 30 July), the *Independent* (https://www.independent.co.uk/news/uk/home-news/prison-sentences-attorney-general-unduly-lenient-sentence-scheme-rapist-murderer-terror-offences-a7867351.html).

1. What is the Unduly Lenient Sentence Scheme?
2. How many prison terms were increased in England and Wales in 2016 as a result of this scheme? Are these figures higher or lower than the previous year?
3. Write down examples of unduly lenient sentences from the article.
4. What conclusions can be drawn with regards to sentencing here?

Link to brief

Gareth Hughes

Your task is to draw objective conclusions about the verdict in the assignment brief. Refer to the assignment brief and the information sources attached to the brief to consider all issues.

CHECKLIST – HAVE YOU INCLUDED:

- [ ] objective conclusions on criminal cases, using evidence and clear reasoning/argument in support of them
- [ ] just verdicts, miscarriage of justice, safe verdicts and just sentencing
- [ ] case examples
- [ ] links to the assignment brief where relevant?

Remember to draw objective conclusions throughout this AC.

CONCLUSION

UNIT 4
CRIME AND PUNISHMENT

AC1.1 DESCRIBE PROCESSES USED FOR LAW-MAKING

See pages 204–207 of the textbook.

In this AC it is important to appreciate the role of the government and the judiciary in how they make law. The law that they make produces the rules of our criminal law.

Exam tip

The process of making domestic legislation is often covered by law students who will go into great detail about the different stages that occur during the parliamentary process. Such detail is not required for this qualification.

Explore online

Watch the YouTube video clip '6 Legislation and Judge Make Law' by the Victorian Law Reform (https://www.youtube.com/watch?v=x0e8cJkUTEU) to understand the differences between parliamentary and judge-made law.

Government process

Explore online

Watch the video clip 'Making Laws' on the parliament.uk website (https://www.parliament.uk/education/about-your-parliament/how-laws-are-made/) and make a brief summary of law-making by Parliament.

Parliament comprises the House of Commons, House of Lords and the Monarch.

Activity 4.1

To help you understand some important terms in the process of government law-making, write a sentence using each of the following terms:

Bill   debate

proposal   Commons   Lords

legislation   Monarch

democratic   Act

The role of the Monarch in law-making is mainly symbolic.

Exam tip ✔

In an exam answer about government law-making, try to include one or two of the parliamentary law-making stages such as first reading second reading, committee stage or report stage.

Take it further ≫

If you find government law-making interesting, especially from a constitutional viewpoint, watch 'An Introduction to Parliament' on YouTube (https://www.youtube.com/embed/RAMbIz3Y2JA) to gain an understanding of how our Parliament was established, is organised and is held to account.

Judicial process of law-making

While the majority of our laws are made through Parliament, senior judges also play a part in law-making. A judge contributes to law-making through (i) judicial precedent and (ii) statutory interpretation. The key points of each are in the following table.

Judges play a part in law-making.

Key terms

Judicial: belonging or related to a judge.

Precedent: a decision in a legal case that must be followed in similar future cases.

Exam tip ✔

Read an exam question carefully to see if it is about a judge participating in law-making or the general role of a judge. The latter will include passing sentences and ruling on issues of law. Such information would not receive credit in this AC.

Type of law-making	Judicial precedent	Statutory interpretation
How it works	Judges must follow decisions from previous similar cases; known as common law. Following the decision is compulsory when it is given by a higher court. Where there is no similar past decision the judge must decide the case and make an original precedent. In doing this they make laws.	If a word or phrase is unclear, a judge must decide its meaning. Judges in higher courts bind (compel to follow) those in lower courts. Such lower courts must follow the interpretation of senior judges.
Examples	*Donoghue* v *Stevenson* was followed by *Daniels* v *White*.	The case of *Whitely* v *Chappell* was decided using the literal rule.
Techniques involved	Judges can also avoid following precedents under certain conditions such as distinguishing, overruling and reversing.	Judges can use different rules of interpretation and in doing so can establish new laws. For example, the literal, golden and mischief rules are rules of interpretation.

Example questions

Previous exam questions on this AC are:

Outline the process used by the government for making laws such as the Theft Act 1968. [3 marks] **Unit 4 2018 exam paper**

Describe judicial involvement in law-making. [4 marks] **Unit 4 2018 exam paper**

Using the mark scheme below, consider how many marks the answers on the following page should receive. Then check your view with the suggested answer online.

0 marks: Nothing worthy of any marks.

1–2 marks: Answers provide a basic description of judicial involvement in law-making. Answers convey meaning but lack detail. Little or no use of specialist vocabulary.

3–4 marks: Answers provide in detail a description of judicial involvement in law-making. Answers communicate meaning with some use of specialist vocabulary.

For more on *Whitely* v *Chappel* see page 207 of the textbook.

For more on *Donoghue* v *Stevenson* and *Daniels* v *White* see page 206 of the textbook.

Exam tip ✔

Details of the finer working of judicial precedent and statutory interpretation are not needed, unlike an exam in A Level Law.

Exam tip ✔

Make sure you understand the difference between government law-making and judicial law-making. Writing about the wrong process in an exam will result in zero marks.

Sample answers

Answer 1

Judges must follow past decisions given by previous courts. Lower courts must follow higher courts and give the same decision in similar cases Only where there is no previous similar decision can a court create a new law.

Answer 2

Judges can make precedents or judge-made law in legal cases. Such decisions are followed in future cases. For example, the tort of negligence was judge-made law, which stated that companies need to take responsibility for negligence and look out for easily available safety standards.

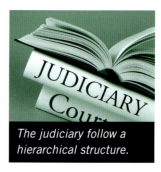

The judiciary follow a hierarchical structure.

Test yourself

1. Can you state two stages of parliamentary law-making?
2. What is a piece of proposed law called?
3. Give the name of a case that shows judicial precedent.
4. Give the name of a case where statutory interpretation took place.
5. In which courts is statutory interpretation carried out?

Take it further

Go to the LawTeacher website and read 'Judicial Precedent Lecture 1' (https://www.lawteacher.net/lecture-notes/judicial-precedent-1.php), then write one sentence explaining the terms *ratio decidendi* and *obiter dicta*.

Exam tip

If you have to answer a question on judge-made law, try to make reference to both judicial precedent and statutory interpretation.

CHECKLIST – ARE YOU ABLE TO:

☐ describe how government/Parliament make laws

☐ describe how judges make law through judicial precedent and statutory interpretation?

AC1.2 DESCRIBE THE ORGANISATION OF THE CRIMINAL JUSTICE SYSTEM IN ENGLAND AND WALES

For this AC you need to know:

- The agencies involved in the Criminal Justice System.
- How they fit into the organisation of the criminal system.
- The relationships between different agencies.
- The extent of cooperation that exists between the different agencies.

The courts

Activity 4.2

Watch 'How Does Britain Work? – the Justice System' on YouTube (https://www.youtube.com/watch?v=aL4ENsRhWzw) and answer the following questions:

1. Where do we find most of our law?

2. Why might law not produce a just result?

3. What types of criminal cases do magistrates deal with?

4. How many criminal cases start in the Magistrates' Court?

5. What percentage of cases are tried in the Magistrates' Court?

6. What is wrong with this statement: 'Magistrates are legally qualified and receive a salary'?

7. What are the types of judges that sit in a Crown Court?

8. What are the names of the three divisions of the High Court?

9. Where is the Court of Appeal situated?

10. What is the name of the highest court in the UK?

Exam tip ✔

You need to be able to show how the agencies are connected to each other. Do not treat them as separate disjointed agencies but rather focus on the relationship or connections that exist.

It is important to show how the agencies in the criminal justice system are connected to each other.

Explore online

Read the information in the press release 'Minister Announces "10 Prisons Project" to Develop New Model of Excellence' on the gov.uk website (https://www.gov.uk/government/news/minister-announces-10-prisons-project-to-develop-new-model-of-excellence) to discover the government's plans to develop a new model of excellence for Britain's prisons. Prepare a summary of the plans and what they aim to implement regarding the problems facing the prison service in achieving social control.

The police service

Relationships between the police service and other agencies in the Criminal Justice System are shown in the table below.

Police service				
CPS	Prison service	Courts	MAPPA (multi-agency public protection arrangements)	Probation service
The police seek advice from the CPS on the charging of suspects. Both agencies work together in the prosecuting of offenders. The CPS offers the police CPS Direct – a 24-hour advice line.	Assist with arrangements to ensure those sentenced to custody are taken there. Police will arrest a prisoner if recalled on licence (breaks the terms of release and must return to prison). It is usually an independent agency that escorts prisoners to prison, e.g. G4S.	Ensure defendants in police custody are before the court.\n\nPolice attend court to give evidence.\n\nPolice apply to the courts for search and arrest warrants.	The police work with the probation and prison services, sharing information with other agencies to assess and manage violent and sexual offenders in order to protect the public from harm.	Both agencies work together in the management of an offender. This includes sharing of information and attending meetings.

Take it further

Research the Multi-Agency Public Protection Arrangements (MAPPA) to appreciate how the agencies in the Criminal Justice System come together to ensure the protection of the public.

Exam tip

The exam question may focus on specific agencies within the Criminal Justice System or allow you to select the agencies.

The police are a main agency in the organisation of the Criminal Justice System and have links with all the other agencies.

Example questions

Describe the relationship of the prison service with other agencies in the Criminal Justice System. [7 marks] **Unit 4 2017 exam paper**

This question allows you to select the agencies you want to consider as working alongside the prison service.

Describe relationships between the police, the Crown Prosecution Service and the courts as a case proceeds through the Criminal Justice System. [6 marks] **Unit 4 2018 exam paper**

This question is very precise regarding the agencies you need to write about.

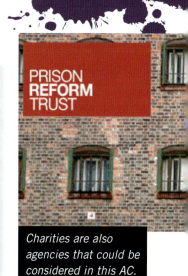

PRISON **REFORM** TRUST

Charities are also agencies that could be considered in this AC.

Sample answer

According to the mark scheme, for the 2018 question, this is the type of information that must go in an answer:

The police will investigate a potential crime and liaise with the CPS regarding charge. The police will ensure arrested suspects held in police custody are brought before the courts. They will also arrest a prisoner recalled whilst on probation and ensure their return to prison.

The CPS will advise the police during the early stages of an investigation. They will review cases submitted by the police for prosecution, prepare cases for court and present those cases at court. In each case reviewed, the prosecutor will consider whether there is sufficient evidence and, if so, whether the public interest requires a prosecution.

The CPS will also carry out the advocacy for hearings in either the Magistrates' Court or the Crown Court.

All cases will start in the Magistrates' Court, with summary offences staying there for determination. Either-way cases, where trial by jury is selected, all indictable offences will proceed to the Crown Court.

Synoptic link

In Unit 3 Crime Scene to Courtroom, you will have studied agencies involved in criminal investigations and can draw on that knowledge to help you answer a question on this AC.

Formal punishment

The Sentencing Council for England and Wales produces guidelines on sentencing for the judiciary and other criminal justice professionals. These guidelines try to ensure that the punishment fits the crime and that sentences are consistent throughout the country. For each crime there is a range of sentences available and a judge or magistrate must decide the correct sentence by taking into account factors such as:

- seriousness of the offence
- harm caused to the victim
- offender's level of blame
- previous convictions of the offender
- personal circumstances of the offender including a guilty plea.

Remember Unit 1 and the campaigns for change? There are campaigns that focus on reform of the Criminal Justice System or rehabilitation of offenders. Such campaign groups have relationships or connections with various agencies. One charity that campaigns to improve the prison system is the Prison Reform Trust. According to its website it is an 'independent charity working to create a just, humane and effective penal system. This is done by inquiring into the workings of the system, informing prisoners, staff and the wider public, and influencing government and officials towards reform.' The work of charities in social control will be further developed in this unit; however, they can also be included in an answer to this AC.

Sentencing Council

The Sentencing Council tries to increase public understanding of sentencing.

Explore online

Go to the Sentencing Council website (https://www.sentencingcouncil.org.uk/offences/) and search for the guidelines for common assault, fraud and grievous bodily harm (s. 20). Compare and contrast the guidelines.

Synoptic link

Charities and other agencies in the Criminal Justice System

CHECKLIST – ARE YOU ABLE TO:

☐ describe the organisation of the Criminal Justice System

☐ describe how the agencies are connected to each other or explain their relationship as a case proceeds through the court?

AC1.3 DESCRIBE MODELS OF CRIMINAL JUSTICE

See pages 213–216 of the textbook.

This AC requires an understanding of two models of justice: namely, the due process and crime control models. These models were put forward by Herbert Packer, a Stanford University law professor. You must be able to describe each model and how it explains justice. Real-life cases to support the points would benefit an answer.

Key term

Model: a system or a procedure used as an example to follow.

The crime control model

This model emphasises the reduction of crime by increased police powers and action with a focus on providing justice for the victim.

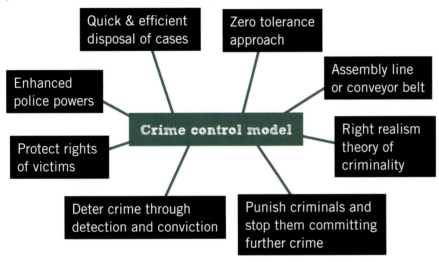

- Quick & efficient disposal of cases
- Zero tolerance approach
- Enhanced police powers
- Assembly line or conveyor belt
- **Crime control model**
- Right realism theory of criminality
- Protect rights of victims
- Deter crime through detection and conviction
- Punish criminals and stop them committing further crime

Exam tip

The specifications do not require you to evaluate the models or decide which one is superior. However, you may be asked to describe a model from the text provided in an exam question.

Synoptic link

Remember the case of Colin Stagg from Unit 3 or the Unit 3 Brief of Gareth Hughes? Consider if any of the points could relate to them.

The due process model

This model focuses on the liberties of the individual and protecting their rights. It would suggest a reduction in police and government powers.

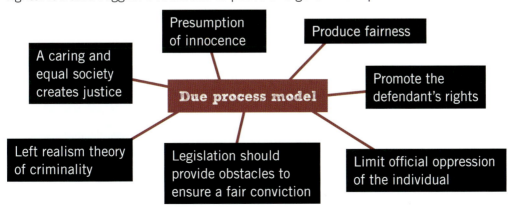

- Presumption of innocence
- Produce fairness
- A caring and equal society creates justice
- **Due process model**
- Promote the defendant's rights
- Left realism theory of criminality
- Legislation should provide obstacles to ensure a fair conviction
- Limit official oppression of the individual

Example question

Colin Chesterton from Newcastle claims that he has been wrongfully convicted of the charge of murder. He was found guilty by a jury at Crown Court with a unanimous verdict. He intends to appeal his conviction, and his family have started a campaign called 'Free the Newcastle One'. Colin claims the police failed to consider any other suspect, and the jury were bribed to find him guilty. In addition, he believes the judge is related to the victim, and this is why he was given the sentence of life imprisonment with a recommendation that he serves 70 years.

Describe how one model of criminal justice could apply to Colin's case. [6 marks] **Unit 4 2018 exam paper**

The mark scheme states the following:

0 marks: Nothing worthy of any marks.

1–3 marks: Answers describe in basic detail how one model of criminal justice could apply to Colin's case. Answers convey meaning but lack detail. Little or no use of specialist vocabulary.

4–6 marks: Answers describe in detail how one model of criminal justice could apply to Colin's case. Answers communicate meaning with some use of specialist vocabulary.

Answers may include:

- The most appropriate model for Colin's case is the crime control model.
- This involves the repression of crime being the most important function of criminal justice because order is a necessary condition for a free society. Colin's claims about the police action would be relevant here.
- Criminal justice should concentrate on promoting victims' rights rather than on protecting defendants' rights. This could account for the judge giving such a harsh sentence as, according to Colin, he is related to the victim.

Take it further

Consider some of the criminal cases featured in the previous three units and decide which ones could fall under the crime control model of justice and which ones fall under the due process model.

Exam tip ✔

Try to link the models of justice to a criminological theory. For example, crime control model links to right realism and due process to left realism.

The image in this picture is known as Lady Justice and is famous for being on top of the Old Bailey in London. She portrays morality and justice in the legal system.

- The criminal justice process should operate like an assembly line conveyor belt, moving cases swiftly along towards their disposition. This could account for Colin's claim that the police failed to consider other suspects.
- If the police make an arrest and a prosecutor files criminal charges, the accused should be presumed guilty because the fact-finding of police and prosecutors is highly reliable. This could explain Colin's claims about his case.
- The due process model with links to Colin's case.

Sample answer

How many marks would you give the following answer? Compare your view with the one online.

The crime control model of justice can be applied to Colin's case. This model states that all defendants are guilty unless they can prove their innocence. The police and other agencies in the Criminal Justice System should have more powers to prove the defendant's guilt no matter what the evidence. This can be seen in Colin's case as all the agencies have clearly done everything in their power to establish a guilty verdict. This applies, despite the fact that he says he is innocent. This model is more concerned with bringing in a guilty verdict as quickly as possible, so the next case can be considered, rather similar to an assembly line. The crime control model focuses on the rights of the victim rather than those of the defendant, It follows a zero tolerance approach where the defendant should be punished for all crime no matter how small.

The crime control and due process models are two conflicting theories of justice.

Activity 4.3

The following are areas of law that support either the crime control model or the due process model. You need to decide which fits each theory of justice.

1. The extended pre-charge detention time for suspected terrorist suspects.
2. The acknowledgement of the need for police procedural safeguards by the introduction of the Police and Criminal Evidence Act 1984.
3. The Human Rights Act 1998 allows for criminal justice practices to be thoroughly looked at from a human rights perspective.
4. The removal of the double jeopardy rule for murder and other serious offences.
5. Allowing the introduction of 'bad character' evidence and previous convictions information for the courts to consider when deliberating a verdict.
6. All police interviews are now recorded and suspects have the right to legal representation.

The answers to this activity can be found in the textbook on pages 214–215.

Activity 4.4

In class, try to act out a police arrest and interview scene. However, first write a script that shows the crime control model and then a second similar script but with a focus on actions under the due process model.

Test yourself

1. Who constructed the two models of justice?
2. Explain areas of law which show the due process model of justice.
3. State a criminological theory linked to the due process model of justice.
4. State a criminological theory linked to crime control.
5. Identify a case that shows aspects of the crime control model.

CHECKLIST – ARE YOU ABLE TO:

- [ ] describe the crime control model of justice
- [ ] describe the due process model of justice
- [ ] describe from text a model of justice?

DUE PROCESS

AC2.1 EXPLAIN FORMS OF SOCIAL CONTROL

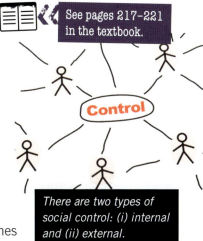

See pages 217–221 in the textbook.

Social control can be internal or external and both types try to regulate the occurrence of crime. This is done by putting forward measures and influences to control the illegal actions of people.

Internal forms of social control

These relate to the thoughts and views that we have regarding crime. As we grow and are influenced by people and situations, we develop morals and codes of behaviour that determine our reaction to crime. Sometimes called a moral compass, it is our conscience that determines whether we abide by the law or commit crime.

There are two types of social control: (i) internal and (ii) external.

Internal forms of social control					
Religion	**Upbringing**	**Traditions**	**Conscience**	**Rational ideology**	**Internalisation of social rules**
Religion has a major influence on how we behave, as we are guided by the moral codes it puts forward for us to follow.	Upbringing, especially parental authority, has a major influence on why we abide by the law.	Linked to our upbringing, traditions have conditioned us to know how to behave and not to commit crimes.	Our moral compass or conscience tells us we should not commit crime as it is wrong. Our conscience is also linked to religion, our upbringing and the traditions we uphold.	People have an idea of what is right and what is wrong and therefore they abide by the law. They are able to use internalisation of social rules.	People are able to work out for themselves their social values and what is unacceptable in society, and therefore do not commit crime.

Activity 4.5

In pairs, consider why you feel you should follow rules and not break the law by explaining what internal influences make you act this way?

Synoptic link

Upbringing is linked to the social learning theory and Bandura.

External forms of social control

External controls are outside influences that make us follow the rules and not commit crime. Such influences persuade or compel us to conform to the rules. The following are examples of external control:

- police
- parents
- teachers
- judges
- magistrates
- traffic wardens
- prisons
- religious leaders
- security staff
- CCTV.

Prisons and the police are obvious external forces of social control.

Example question

This question from the **Unit 4 2017 exam paper** asks:

Explain why imprisonment acts as an external form of social control. [4 marks]

The type of information that should go in an answer can be seen in the mark scheme as follows:

0 marks: Nothing worthy of any marks.

1–2 marks: Answers provide a basic/limited explanation of why imprisonment acts as an external form of social control. Answers convey meaning but lack detail. Little or no use of specialist vocabulary.

3–4 marks: Answers provide a detailed explanation of why imprisonment acts as an external form of social control. Answers communicate meaning with some use of specialist vocabulary.

Likely answers may include:

- The threat of imprisonment acts to persuade or compel/coerce members of society to conform to the rules.
- The fear of punishment/possible imprisonment may deter people from offending.
- The idea of a loss of liberty may ensure social control.
- The possibility of a substantial term of imprisonment may deter people from committing serious crimes.
- Fear of the consequences of a prison sentence in future life, such as loss of employment, may act as a social control mechanism.

Exam tip ✔

Use of specialist terminology allows higher marks to be awarded in the exam. In this AC try to include the following terms:
- rational ideology
- tradition
- internalisation of social rules and morality.

Exam tip ✔

If you are asked a question about external social control try to make sure you explain how it acts as coercion or a compelling force, also how it provides a fear of punishment and a deterrence for both the general public and the individual.

Control theory

The control theory explains why people do not commit crime. This involves the view that people do not commit criminal or deviant acts because there are factors that control their behaviour and desire or impulse to break the rules. Two theorists that should be considered are Walter C. Reckless and Travis Hirschi.

For more on Reckless and Hirschi see pages 220–221 of the textbook.

Activity 4.6

Below is a summary of each theory. Complete the gaps using the textbook for reference.

Walter C. Reckless

Reckless developed one version of control theory, known as _____. He argued that we can _____ _____ _____ due to inner and _____ containment. Inner containment comes from our _____ and particularly the influence from our _____. Outer containment refers to the influence of _____, including the laws of the society in which we live. A combination of _____ psychological containments and _____ social containments prevents people from deviating from _____ _____.

Travis Hirschi

Hirschi believed that people must form _____ _____ to prevent criminal behaviour. He stated there are four bonds, _____, _____, involvement and _____, and these must be properly formed to prevent a person having a propensity to commit crime. Hirschi's research claimed that _____ attachment to parents, school and a _____ was important to promote pro-social behaviour. In addition, commitment to accomplishing _____ _____ _____ such as a good job and nice house, etc. was needed. Alongside these, an involvement with some social activity such as playing in a sports team or belonging to a community group is needed to _____ _____ _____.
Finally, what is also needed to ensure people conform to society's rules is a belief in society's values such as _____ and _____ _____ _____.

Properly formed attachments, especially those with parents, are important in Travis Hirschi's control theory.

Activity 4.7

Using the information in this section and the information in the textbook, answer the following question. A good answer will become a very useful revision aid.

Discuss reasons why individuals abide by the law. [8 marks]

Exam tip

Use of specialist terminology allows higher marks to be awarded in the exam. In this AC try to include the following terms:

- coercion
- fear of punishment
- individual deterrence
- general deterrence
- control theory.

CHECKLIST – ARE YOU ABLE TO:

- [ ] give examples of internal social control
- [ ] explain how internal social control prevents crime, using terms such as rational ideology, tradition and internalisation of social rules and morality
- [ ] give examples of external social control
- [ ] explain how external social control prevents crime, using terms such as coercion, fear of punishment, deterrence and control theory
- [ ] briefly explain the theories put forward by Walter C. Reckless and Travis Hirschi?

Conscience

AC2.2 DISCUSS THE AIMS OF PUNISHMENT

See pages 222–228 of the textbook.

In this AC you must be able to discuss the following aims of punishment:

- retribution
- rehabilitation
- deterrence, including prevention of reoffending and deterrence of others from committing similar crimes
- public protection
- reparation.

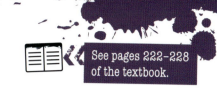

Retribution, as an aim of punishment, has a large element of revenge.

Retribution

Try to give examples of punishments that could be seen to meet the aim being considered. This will be developed further in the next AC. For retribution, punishments such as the death penalty for murder or long prison sentences for serious offences are appropriate. Retributions are not punishment for punishment's sake but the desire to ensure the offender is adequately punished and no more. It does not seek to change behaviour and is often thought of as a backwards-thinking aim.

Exam tip ✓

Retribution is about giving punishment at the right level. When discussing this aim try to use the following terminology:
- just desserts
- revenge
- let the punishment fit the crime
- an eye for an eye.

Explore online ➤

Read the article 'David Cameron: All Sentences Must Have Element of "Punishment"' by Rosa Prince (2012, 22 October), the *Telegraph* (https://www.telegraph.co.uk/news/politics/david-cameron/9625660/David-Cameron-all-sentences-must-have-element-of-punishment.html) and write a short summary of David Cameron's views on the aims of punishment.

Such views and ideas can be included in any question about retribution. Quoting the former Prime Minister's view would attract credit in an exam situation.

Synoptic link

When considering retribution, try to link it to a criminological theory that you studied in Unit 2. Given that retribution is all about punishment, it connects to right realism with the idea of getting tough on crime.

Right realism states that the offender's social bonds are weak and there may well be a poor economic background where the offender is unable to control their criminal urges. Hence, there is a need for punishment to prevent crime.

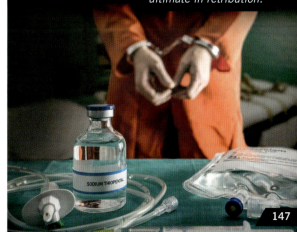

The death penalty for murder is probably the ultimate in retribution.

Rehabilitation

The aim of rehabilitation is almost the opposite of retribution. This aim tries to change the offender and make them use free will or their own mind so that they do not to want to commit crime but rather conform to the rules of society. Hence, it is considered a forward-thinking aim. When considering rehabilitation try to include the following terminology:

- reform
- free will
- community orders.

Try to include punishments that attempt to rehabilitate offenders such as a probation order with conditions including unpaid work or attendance at treatment centres for issues such as drugs or alcohol. These orders try to educate and change the offenders' views so that they do not want to commit crime. Restorative justice is a good example of offenders recognising that their offending is wrong and changing their mindset as to an appreciation of the consequences of their criminality.

Synoptic link Try to link rehabilitation to a criminological theory from Unit 2. Consider how some individualistic theories promote behaviour modification techniques for changing the way a criminal thinks and acts.

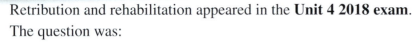
Example question

Retribution and rehabilitation appeared in the **Unit 4 2018 exam**. The question was:

Discuss retribution and rehabilitation as aims of sentencing. [10 marks]

This question wanted a discussion of both aims and could include information such as:
- An explanation of what each term means.
- Examples of punishments that try to meet the aims.
- Key specialist terminology.
- Links to criminological theories.
- Case examples where possible.

Take it further

Research 'The Woolf Within' and use it as an example of successful rehabilitation.

Peter Woolf was rehabilitated using restorative justice.

Sample answer

Following is a sample answer and mark scheme. What would you give this answer?

Retribution is an aim that seeks to give the sentence that best suits the crime. In other words, the punishment must fit the crime. This can be seen in the biblical phrase 'an eye for an eye'. Therefore, smaller offences get smaller punishments. So, for example, anti-social behaviour may be given a Criminal Behaviour Order. Whereas armed robbery will probably get a lengthy prison sentence. Murder would get a life sentence due to the need to protect society. Retribution does not seek to change an offender's behaviour and is a backward-looking policy. It merely seeks revenge for the victim and society. The death penalty for murder is an example of retribution.

Rehabilitation on the other hand does try to change an offender's behaviour and mindset. It is therefore considered a forward-thinking aim. Punishments that try to reform an offender would be considered as rehabilitative and these may include community orders with a condition of a treatment relating to matters such as alcohol or drug abuse.

Armed robbery offenders usually receive a lengthy prison sentence.

Mark scheme

0 marks: Nothing worthy of any marks.

1–4 marks: Answers discuss in basic detail retribution and rehabilitation as aims of sentencing. Answers convey meaning but lack detail. Little or no use of specialist vocabulary.

5–8 marks: Answers discuss in some detail retribution and rehabilitation as aims of sentencing. Answers communicate meaning with some use of specialist vocabulary.

9–10 marks: Answers discuss in detail retribution and rehabilitation as aims of sentencing. Answers are well structured and clearly expressed. Specialist terms are used with ease and accuracy.

Exam tip ✔

Always try to give an example of an actual punishment that links to the aim you are considering.

Deterrence, public protection, reparation and denunciation

Following is a table with the main points about the aims on the previous page. Make sure that you understand the summaries and can include each column's information in an exam answer.

Denunciation is society's way of expressing disapproval of the crime.

Aim	Explanation	Examples of punishment	Link to theory	Terminology
Deterrence	Trying to dissuade the offender with both general and individual fear of punishment.	General – long prison sentences, e.g. London rots 2011. Individual — suspended sentence.	Social learning theory – trying to learn not to reoffend or sometimes learning from others to better criminal traits.	Fear of punishment
Public protection	Keeping society safe from dangerous people.	Typically, custodial sentences including a life sentence but also driving disqualification, probation and chemical castration.	Right realism being tough on crime.	Incapacitation
Reparation	Providing compensation for the crime or repairing the wrong done.	Community orders with an unpaid work element or compensation for offences such as criminal damage or assault.	Left realism and the use of practical measures to prevent crime.	Remorse Community payback
Denunciation	Reinforcing rules, including moral and ethical ideas. E.g., the community came together following the abduction of Shannon Matthews.	Prison sentences for sexual or violent offences showing that society will not tolerate such behaviour.	Functionalism to show that crime serves a purpose.	Boundary maintenance Disapproval

Activity 4.8

Read online 'UK Knife Crime Offenders Getting Longer Jail Sentences', an article from the *Guardian* by Damien Gayle (2018, 8 March) (https://www.theguardian.com/uk-news/2018/mar/08/uk-knife-crime-offenders-longer-jail-sentences). Consider which aims of punishment could be achieved by the sentences discussed.

Test yourself

1. State a punishment that tries to achieve rehabilitation.
2. Which aim of punishment is said to be 'an eye for an eye'?
3. Which aim of punishment could be both general and individual?
4. The social learning theory could link to which aim of punishment?
5. State a case where society showed its denunciation.
6. Explain what is meant by reparation.
7. Is retribution a forward- or backward-looking aim?
8. Which aims of punishment might a prison sentence achieve?

Take it further

Read the article 'Why Doesn't Prison Work for Women' on the BBC News website (https://www.bbc.co.uk/news/uk-england-45627845) and consider the impact of short-term prison sentences. This leads into the next AC.

CHECKLIST – ARE YOU ABLE TO:

☐ discuss the following aims of punishments:

- retribution
- rehabilitation
- deterrence
- public protection
- reparation

☐ link aims of punishment to criminological theories from Unit 2?

AC2.3 ASSESS HOW FORMS OF PUNISHMENT MEET THE AIMS OF PUNISHMENT

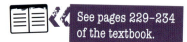

See pages 229–234 of the textbook.

Activity 4.9

Match the punishment to the description.

A	Discharge	**1.**	Can be a combination order such as unpaid work, curfew or supervision.
B	Imprisonment	**2.**	Depends on the financial circumstances of the offender.
C	Fines	**3.**	Are generally conditional but can be absolute.
D	Community service	**4.**	Are generally fixed term but can be suspended or for life.

Imprisonment

Imprisonment has several aims, including:

- **Retribution**: to achieve revenge for the crime. Murder, for instance, carries a mandatory life sentence, showing that the punishment fits the crime.

- **Rehabilitation**: it would be hoped that the offender's mindset is changed and they no longer want to commit crime.

- **Deterrence**: if an offender has been to prison they may not want to return and are therefore deterred from criminality. Also, prison may be a general deterrence to society as it may put people off committing offences because they cannot face going to prison.

- **Public protection/incapacitation**: prison is generally reserved for the most dangerous offenders, as their incarceration keeps them apart from and hence protects the public.

- **Denunciation**: when an offender is sent to prison it can be seen as an act on behalf of society to show that they disapprove of the crime and that it is deserving of a serious sentence.

Now we know which aims imprisonment could achieve we have to make a judgement about whether or not the aims are actually achieved.

Explore online

Read 'Can Prison Work?' by Prisoner Ben (2015, 21 December) on the *Guardian* website (https://www.theguardian.com/commentisfree/2015/dec/21/can-prison-work-crime) and write a summary of the view of the writer about prison in no more than five sentences.

A custodial sentence can achieve many aims of punishment.

All the following facts are from 'Prison: The Facts: Bromley Briefings Summer 2018' by the Prison Reform Trust (http://www.prisonreformtrust.org.uk/Portals/0/Documents/Bromley%20Briefings/Summer%202018%20factfile.pdf).

England and Wales has the highest imprisonment rate in Western Europe.

The prison population has risen by 77% in the last 30 years.

65,000 people were sent to prison to serve a sentence in 2017.

Short prison sentences are less effective than community sentences at reducing reoffending.

People serving mandatory life sentences are spending more of their sentence in prison. On average they spend 17 years in custody, up from 13 years in 2001.

Many of our prisons are overcrowded – and have been for a long time. Overcrowding affects whether activities, staff and other resources are available to reduce risk of reoffending, as well as distance from families and other support networks.

Many are released from prison, only to return there shortly after.

The number of people recalled back to custody has increased, particularly amongst women. 8,825 people serving a sentence of less than 12 months were recalled to prison in the year to December 2017.

Prison has a poor record for reducing reoffending – nearly half of adults (48%) are reconvicted within one year of release. For those serving sentences of less than 12 months this increases to 64%.

NOTE: the Bromley Briefings are produced in memory of Keith Bromley, and are produced in conjunction with the charity Prison Reform Trust.

Given the above, it could be argued that, as so many people are sent to prison, retribution is achieved. For the time the offenders are in prison, public protection is also achieved. However, given the reoffending rates, rehabilitation does not appear to be successful.

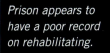

Prison appears to have a poor record on rehabilitating.

Community orders are considered more successful than a custodial sentence. (Photograph courtesy of Working Links)

Do community sentences achieve the aims of punishment?

Community sentences, which include probation supervision, can include one or more of the following:

- community payback (unpaid work for 40–300 hours)
- treatment and programmes (to help with addictions and mental health issues)
- restrictions such as a curfew, electronic tag or residence condition.

Short prison sentences are less effective than community sentences at reducing reoffending. People serving prison sentences of less than 12 months had a reoffending rate seven percentage points higher than similar offenders serving a community sentence – they also committed more crimes.

Community sentences are particularly effective for people who have a large number of previous offences. For those with more than 50 previous offences, the odds of reoffending are more than a third higher (36%) when a short prison sentence is used rather than a community sentence. **(Prison Reform Trust, 'Prison: The Facts: Bromley Briefings Summer 2018)**

From the above, it could be argued that community sentences have a degree of success in achieving rehabilitation. Reparation may be achieved by community payback.

Activity 4.10

Nominate a community payback project to suggest what unpaid work is carried out by offenders in your local area. See the Nominate a Community Payback Project, on the gov.uk website (https://www.gov.uk/nominate-community-payback-project).

Take it further

Provide a brief summary considering if financial penalties achieve any aims of sentencing. The following online articles will provide you will some ideas:

- 'Unpaid Court Fines Approach £2bn' (2012, 20 March), BBC News (https://www.bbc.co.uk/news/uk-politics-17438873).
- 'Hampshire Criminals Rack up £16m in Unpaid Court Fines' (2015, 11 February), *Gazette* (http://www.basingstokegazette.co.uk/news/crime/11785452.Hampshire_criminals_rack_up___16m_in_unpaid_court_fines/).

Test yourself

1. Can you explain the various conditions that could be attached to a community order?
2. Can you provide statistics on reoffending?
3. Who oversees a probation order?
4. What is restorative justice?
5. What types of sentences achieve public protection?

Take it further

Invite a visitor from an agency of social control into your centre to discuss their role. Possible areas include:

- police
- magistrates
- prison system
- probation service
- Crown Prosecution Service
- a local charity.

CHECKLIST – ARE YOU ABLE TO:

- [ ] assess aims that are achieved by imprisonment
- [ ] assess aims that are achieved by a community order
- [ ] assess aims that achieved by financial penalties
- [ ] assess aims that are achieved by discharges?

LEARNING OUTCOME 3 UNDERSTAND MEASURES USED IN SOCIAL CONTROL

AC3.1 EXPLAIN THE ROLE OF AGENCIES IN SOCIAL CONTROL

See pages 235–245 of the textbook.

You should be able to answer a question on the role of the following agencies:

- police
- CPS
- judiciary
- prisons
- probation service
- charities and pressure groups.

The role of the police in achieving social control

What constitutes the role of the police is outlined in the specifications and includes aspects shown in the following mind map.

Specialist operations: include anti-terrorism, mounted police, dog handlers, drug unit, armed response

Working practices: work across the country, dealing with all types of criminality. Responsibilities include: general beat duties; emergency and non-emergency calls from the public; neighbourhood officers; the Criminal Investigation Department (CID)

Funding: central government grant and through council tax

There are 39 **police forces** in England and 4 in Wales

Police powers: include search, arrest, detention and interview. The main law for police powers is the Police and Criminal Evidence Act 1984

The role of the Crown Prosecution Service (CPS) in achieving social control

See pages 238–239 of the textbook.

The CPS is the principal prosecuting agency in England and Wales.

Activity 4.11

Using the textbook to help, answer the following questions on the role of the CPS:

1. Name the act that established the CPS.
2. How is the CPS funded?
3. List the tasks of the CPS, with particular reference to how they work with the police.
4. What are the values of the CPS?
5. Explain how the CPS is organised.
6. Describe the tests used by the CPS to decide whether or not to charge a suspect.

Synoptic link

This links to Unit 3 AC2.1, which requires you to explain the requirements of the CPS for prosecuting suspects.

The role of the judiciary in achieving social control

Philosophy: judges take an Oath of Allegiance (to the Crown) and a Judicial Oath

Judicial independence ensures the law is applied equally in all cases and without bias

Judges are appointed and not elected

Working practices: judges are divided into:

(i) **Superior judges** (working in the High Court and above)

(ii) **Inferior judges** (working in the lower courts)

Aims and objectives: to ensure appropriate management of the trial and ensure it is human rights compliant. Advise the jury on the law and sum up the case evidence for them

In **appeal cases** such as those in the Court of Appeal and the Supreme Court a superior will interpret the law and decide on the application of law to case facts

Funding: the Senior Salaries Review Body (SSRB) recommend judicial salaries to the Prime Minister and Lord Chancellor

Example question

Following is an exam question on the judiciary from the **Unit 4 2017 exam paper**:

Describe the role of the judge in a Crown Court trial. [4 marks]

Here are some points of answer:

- The system is adversarial, which means that the parties run their cases, with the judge acting as referee.
- The judge has to ensure, as far as possible, that the jury understands the evidence and the issues.
- The judge will deal with any points of law that have to be decided and advise the jury on how to apply the law to whatever facts they find.
- The judge will advise the jury on procedure and explain their duties.
- The judge will ensure a fair trial and ensure it is human rights compliant.
- The judge will pass sentence if the defendant is found guilty.
- Under the Criminal Justice Act 2003, it is possible for a judge to sit alone, without a jury, to determine a verdict.

Explore online

Using the parliamament.uk website 'Judicial Role' page (https://www.parliament.uk/about/living-heritage/evolutionofparliament/houseoflords/judicialrole/), investigate how the judicial role of Parliament has functioned and evolved since the 14th century.

A judge oversees a Crown Court trial and advises the jury on the law.

The role of the prison service in achieving social control

Role of Her Majesty's Prison (HMP) Service	To keep those sentenced to prison in custody, helping them lead law-abiding and useful lives both while they are in prison and after they are released.
Who does the prison service work with?	The courts, police, probation service and charities.
How are prisons funded?	Most are funded by the government through taxation. A small number are run and funded by private organisations, e.g. HMP Northumberland.

PRISON

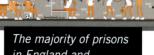

The majority of prisons in England and Wales are run by the government.

(Continued)

What are the categories of prison?	Category A: high/maximum security, e.g. HMP Frankland. Category B: high risk to others, e.g. HMP Durham. Category C: lower risk but not trusted to be in open conditions, e.g. HMP Berwyn. Category D: very low risk to others and due to be released soon, e.g. HMP Kirkham.
The Privilege Scheme inside prisons	Basic level: reduced to this level for bad behaviour. Standard level: level upon entry to prison. Enhanced level: can rise to this level as a reward with extra privileges.

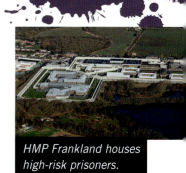

HMP Frankland houses high-risk prisoners.

Example question

Outline the role of the prison service in England and Wales.
[3 marks] **Unit 4 2018 exam paper**

Explore online

Watch the 'HMP Berwyn, Wrexham's New Prison' video on YouTube to learn about Britain's newest prison (https://www.youtube.com/watch?v=ZtruGA5QQnE).

Sample answers

Answer A

The prison service is there to rehabilitate offenders by providing rehabilitation programmes to help them reform. They also provide education and have to follow the human rights to keep prisoners safe.

Answer B

The prison service is responsible for keeping and taking care of prisoners They may also provide rehabilitation services to reform prisoners. Prisons are generally funded by the government but some are privately maintained.

Answer C

The prison service must keep prisoners safe and secure within custody. It also provides protection to the public during the time the offenders are in prison. They try to rehabilitate the offenders so that they can lead law-abiding lives when they are released. They work closely with other agencies in the Criminal Justice System such as courts and the probation service. Most of the prisons are funded through the government but some are privately run.

Answers A and B are worth **2/3** marks and the more detailed and better written answer C would receive full marks **3/3**. You should note that if the question was worth more marks such as 5 or 6 much more detail would be required.

The role of the probation service in achieving social control

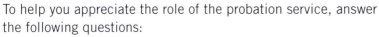
Activity 4.12

To help you appreciate the role of the probation service, answer the following questions:

1. What category of prisoners do the National Probation Service oversee?
2. What are the community rehabilitation companies?
3. How does a probation order work?
4. What is the rule about prisoners leaving prison and probation?
5. What requirements might be placed on a probation order?
6. How is the National Probation Service funded?
7. How are community rehabilitation companies funded?
8. Can you give some examples of the type of work carried out by those on probation?

All the answers can be found in the textbook page 243.

Take it further

Read 'Private Probation Companies to Have Contracts Ended Early' by Jamie Grierson (2018, 27 July), the *Guardian* (https://www.theguardian.com/society/2018/jul/27/private-probation-companies-contracts-ended-early-justice) and get a head start for AC3.4. Make notes about the changes to the running of probation through the community rehabilitation companies.

Example question

Explain the role of the National Probation Service in achieving social control. [4 marks] **Unit 4 2017 exam paper**

Sample answer

Here is a **4/4** answer:

The National Probation Service aims to protect the public by the effective rehabilitation of high-risk offenders. They try to get offenders to turn their lives around by tackling the causes of offending. They manage approved premises for offenders with a residence requirement. Funded by the government, they work with the courts by preparing pre-sentence reports. They liaise with prisons assessing offenders to prepare them for release on licence into the community, when they will come under supervision. They also help all offenders serving sentences in the community to meet the requirements ordered.

The probation service run approved premises where offenders on probation may have to reside.

Test yourself

1. How are the police funded?
2. Name the two tests the CPS use to decide whether or not to charge a suspect.
3. Which agency's aim is to reduce crime and maintain law and order?
4. What types of powers do the police have?
5. How is the CPS funded?
6. Which body recommends the salary of the judiciary?
7. What is the role of a judge in the Crown Court?
8. Who controls the prisons in England and Wales?
9. Can you explain the part privatisation of the probation service, including plans to reverse the decision?
10. What is the main role of the National Probation Service?

The role of charities and pressure groups in achieving social control

Charities and pressure groups are not government agencies but are independent organisations funded through voluntary donations. There are several that work within the Criminal Justice System and it is important that you can explain their role in contributing to achieving social control. You can select any agency you wish but two popular and widely known ones are Prison Reform Trust and Howard League for Penal Reform. You can follow your selected charity or pressure group in the remaining ACs.

Exam tip

It is important to look at the role of charities in achieving social control. A question could appear on the exam paper about them. However, the question will not ask about a specific charity but would be more general to allow any charity or charities to be considered. This allows choice in deciding which one(s) to study.

Prison Reform Trust

Activity 4.13

Look at the Prison Reform Trust website (http://www.prisonreformtrust.org.uk/) and navigate around it to find the answers to the following:

1. Give three of the values and principles that underpin the Prison Reform Trust's work.
2. What are the Prison Reform Trust's main objectives?
3. What type of information can the Prison Reform Trust give prisoners information on?
4. How does the Prison Reform Trust ensure there is a just, humane and effective penal system – one that reserves prison for the most serious offenders, and treats prisoners and their families with the humanity and respect they deserve?
5. How is the Prison Reform Trust funded?
6. Give three examples of the Prison Reform Trust's projects and research areas.

PRISON REFORM TRUST

Prison Reform Trust is a leading charity in prison reform.

Howard League for Penal Reform

Howard League for **Penal Reform**

The oldest penal reform charity in the UK.

Activity 4.14

Go to the Howard League for Penal Reform website (https://howardleague.org/about-us/) and navigate around it to find the answers to the following:

1. When was the charity formed?
2. Who is it named after?
3. What is the main aim of the Howard League for Penal Reform?
4. Briefly explain the campaign about children and policing.
5. How does it help to achieve less crime?
6. How does it help to make communities safer?

Charities are not government funded and rely on donations

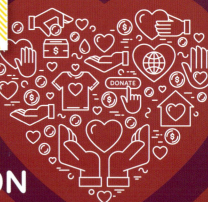

CHARITY & DONATION

Test yourself

1. Which agencies of social control are government funded?
2. Name three specialist roles in the police service.
3. How many police forces are there in England and Wales?
4. Name the tests used by the CPS to decide if an offender should be prosecuted.
5. Who recommends salaries for the judiciary?
6. In which courts do superior judges work?
7. What are the categories of prison?
8. Name a privately run prison.
9. What are community rehabilitation companies and which agency are they linked to?
10. Explain the role of a charity working in the social control sector.

Activity 4.15

Go to http://www.unlock.org.uk/ and answer the following questions about the charity 'Unlock'.

1. Who do the charity help?
2. What type of help does it provide?
3. How many people people are there in the UK with a criminal record?

Click on to the 'Issues, policies and campaigns' section and view the type of work the charity does.

CHECKLIST – ARE YOU ABLE TO:

☐ explain the role of the police in achieving social control

☐ explain the role of the Crown Prosecution Service in achieving social control

☐ explain the role of the judiciary in achieving social control

☐ explain the role of prisons in achieving social control

☐ explain the role of charities and pressure groups in achieving social control?

AC3.2 DESCRIBE THE CONTRIBUTION OF AGENCIES TO ACHIEVING SOCIAL CONTROL

 See pages 246–254 of the textbook.

For this AC the specifications require the contribution of agencies to be described in a particular way. This includes:

- environmental tactics trying to achieve social control
- behavioural tactics trying to achieve social control
- institutional disciplinary procedures such as staged sanction systems
- gaps that result in achieving social control.

Key term

Environment: the surroundings in which a person lives.

Dense foliage can obscure a view and could conceal potential criminals.

Environmental design

Environmental design relates to the design of outside space or even buildings to reduce crime. Make sure you are familiar with tactics used in the design of the environment. Crime prevention through environmental design (CPTED) was introduced by C. Ray Jeffery.

Crime prevention through environmental design (CPTED)			
Prevent opportunities for crime to take place by altering the physical environment			
Aspects of the environment that could encourage crime	Aspects of the environment that will help prevent crime	Explanation	Additional information from the Explore online activity
Dense, full spaces	Open space	Potential offenders can be seen at an early stage and avoidance techniques put in place.	
Poor lighting	Good lighting	Avoiding dark areas allow potential crimes to be pre-empted.	
Obstructed view	Clear visibility	Any object obstructs a view and may cause difficulty by failing to allow someone to appreciate the early warning of a potential crime occurring.	
Places to hide	Nothing that allows someone to hide	Places to hide could encourage a crime to take place.	

(Continued) »

Aspects of the environment that could encourage crime	Aspects of the environment that will help prevent crime	Explanation	Additional information from the Explore online activity
High-level bushes and foliage	Low-level bushes	Low-level bushes and foliage allow visibility and no place to hide.	
Opaque door material	Transparent door material	Knowledge of who is at the door allows a decision whether it is appropriate to open it.	

Go to page 248 of the textbook to read about some of these successes.

Explore online

Watch 'Crime Prevention Through Environmental Design (CPTED)' on YouTube (https://www.youtube.com/watch?v=Xetxsxy1nK8) and add additional information to the table above.

Exam tip

CPTED can be very successful and it will enhance an exam answer if you can add in details of some of its successes.

Prison design

As well as the design of the environment, consideration should also be given to the design of prisons.

Panopticon	Super max	Open prisons	Human ecological prison
All-seeing design with a tower in the centre. Permanent visibility ensures a sense of power. Originally designed by Jeremy Bentham. An example in the UK is HMP Pentonville, London.	Super maximum levels of security for very dangerous criminals, including those who are a threat to national security, e.g. ADX Florence in Colorado USA.	An open prison has minimum restrictions on prisoner movements and activities. Classed as category D prisons, they are generally used to prepare inmates for their release, e.g. HMP Kirkham.	A prison based on making use of human ecology as a method of teaching individuals to discover that they are part of a global community, e.g. Bastøy Prison in Norway.
HMP Pentonville	*ADX Florence, Colorado*	*HMP Kirkham*	*Bastøy Prison, Norway*

Gated lanes

Refer to page 250 of the textbook to help answer these questions if you need help.

Activity 4.16

Answer the following:
1. What are gated lanes?
2. Who has the power to erect the gates?
3. What are some advantages of gated lanes?
4. What are some disadvantages of gated lanes?
5. Give an example of where they are located in the UK.

Take it further

Read 'Norway's Bastoy Prison: A Focus on Human Ecology' by Britton Nagy (2014, 21 November), Pulitzer Center (https://pulitzercenter.org/reporting/norways-bastoy-prison-focus-human-ecology) about Norway's Bastøy Prison and make notes on how it is run.

Take it further

Read the College of Policing's article (2018) 'Alley Gating Systematic Review Published' (http://whatworks.college.police.uk/About/News/Pages/Alley_Gating.aspx) and write a 100-word summary of the main points.

Behavioural tactics

These are tactics to change an offender's behaviour so that they are inclined not to commit offences, as listed in the table on the following page.

Synoptic link
Remember individualistic theories from Unit 2 and the connection to how an individual learns from life experiences. Such a theory can show how crime can be controlled.

Gated lanes may reduce crime in an area.

Anti-social behaviour

Anti Social Behaviour Order (ASBO)/replaced by Criminal Behaviour Order (CBO)	ASBOs no longer exist, having been replaced by CBOs. They were beset with issues including persistent breaches and offenders viewing them as a badge of honour. A CBO can prohibit an offender from doing something detailed in an order that causes harassment, alarm or distress, or from doing a preparatory act that could produce offending, e.g. prevent an offender from entering a particular area. Alternatively, there could be a positive condition such as attendance at a course on alcohol abuse or a step to address the underlying cause of the offending.
Token economy	Based on the principle of rewarding positive behaviour and punishing negative behaviour. A list of desirable behaviours is produced, as is a list of behaviours that should be avoided. A reward is provided for positive behaviour, which can be exchanged for something desired.

Disciplinary procedures and institutional tactics

Some institutions have their own rules and guidance on how to maintain control within their organisation. One of the main institutions is prison. A list of prison rules and the consequences of breaking them can be found on the Prison Reform Trust's website (http://www.prisonreformtrust.org.uk/Portals/0/Documents/PIB%20extract%20-%20Prison%20rules.pdf).

 Activity 4.17

Using the Prison Reform Trust's website, make brief notes of the differences in punishments for adult offenders and young offenders.

Prison rules	
Action that breaks the rules	**Possible punishment**
<ul><li>Behaving in a way that could offend, threaten or hurt someone else</li><li>Stopping prison staff from doing their jobs</li><li>Escaping from prison</li><li>Taking drugs or alcohol</li><li>Causing damage to the prison or young offender institution</li><li>Not doing what prison staff say to do</li><li>Breaking the rules while out of prison for a short time</li></ul>	<ul><li>May have to spend extra days in prison if the offence is serious enough. Up to a maximum for 42 days for each offence</li><li>Could receive a caution</li><li>Privileges (such as having a TV in the cell) could be taken away for up to 42 days</li><li>Up to 84 days' worth of any money earned could be stopped</li><li>Could be locked in a cell alone, away from other prisoners for up to 35 days</li><li>If on remand, privileges could be taken away</li></ul>

There are other institutions that impose sanctions against their members for inappropriate action. These include professional bodies such as the General Medical Council and FIFA (Fédération Internationale de Football Association).

The **General Medical Council** is the independent regulator for doctors. It is able to:

- give warnings
- accept undertakings (promises)
- refer the matter to the Medical Practitioners' Tribunal Service, which has the power to restrict, suspend or revoke a doctor's registration in the UK.

General Medical Council

Staged sanctions

There are many organisations that use a staged sanction system for rule breaking. For instance, a school may have a system of warnings and intervention at different levels. This could include a discussion, followed by contact with home and ultimately exclusion. Likewise, places of employment may give a verbal warning followed by a written warning and eventually dismissal in appropriate circumstances.

There are times when agencies in the Criminal Justice System have a staged response to crime. If the offence warrants a prosecution then the matter will proceed to court. However, there are times when an out of court disposal may be appropriate.

For instance, the police can issue a 'simple' caution or a formal warning to adults who admit committing an offence. This is designed to dispose of the case without a prosecution if it is in the public interest to do so.

The police can also offer a 'conditional' caution if it is considered that there is sufficient evidence to charge the offender with an offence and that it is in the public interest to offer the conditional caution. The offender must also admit the offence.

In addition, if an offender is on a probation order and there is a minor breach then the offender's manager may well provide a formal warning to deal with the matter rather than a referral to court for breach proceedings. However, if the breaches persist there is likely to be a referral back to court.

Police can offer a 'conditional' caution.

Gaps in provision

Unrecorded crime	Budget cuts

Gaps in provision and reasons for them

Lack of resources	Unreported crime

Synoptic link

In Unit 1 you considered the reasons for and consequences of unreported crime. When this happens social control cannot occur.

Activity 4.18

Using the headings in the mind map on the left for gaps in provision, write three sentences for each explaining their relevance.

Test yourself

1. What does CPTED stand for?
2. Who is credited with the use of CPTED in crime prevention?
3. Give three examples of how the environment can be adjusted to help prevent crime.
4. Explain how the design of a prison may impact on crime control.
5. What are gated lanes?
6. Do gated lanes help prevent crime?
7. Which behavioural tactics can positively impact of crime control?
8. What order replaced ASBOs?
9. State three examples of breaking prison rules and the sanctions that could be imposed as a result.
10. Explain one staged sanction system.
11. State three gaps in provision that can prevent social control being achieved.

CHECKLIST – ARE YOU ABLE TO:

- [ ] describe the environmental tactics used to achieve social control
- [ ] describe the use of gated lanes in crime prevention
- [ ] describe the behavioural tactics used to achieve social control including criminal behaviour orders and token economies
- [ ] describe the institutional and disciplinary tactics used to achieve social control
- [ ] describe examples of staged or phased sanctions
- [ ] describe gaps in state provision?

AC3.3 EXAMINE THE LIMITATIONS OF AGENCIES IN ACHIEVING SOCIAL CONTROL

See pages 255–262 of the textbook.

Limitations are detailed in the exam specifications

- **Repeat offenders/recidivism**: prisoners relapsing into reoffending.
- **Civil liberties and legal barriers**: laws that can be seen as preventing social control.
- **Access to resources and support**: a lack of resources and support can prevent social control being established.
- **Finance**: a lack of funding in many agencies can reduce the effectiveness of social control.
- **Local and national policies**: a focus of policies being enforced in one area may result in a lack of prioritising in another.
- **Environment**: the environment in which an offender lives may not encourage social control.
- **Crime committed by those with moral imperatives**: offenders may commit crimes as they believe it is the correct and moral way to behave.

Key term

Limitations: something that controls or reduces something.

Synoptic link

The criminological theories considered in Unit 2 can be seen in the limitations in achieving social control. The table below shows how they are connected.

Limitation	Theory
Repeat offenders/recidivism: offenders can learn from those around them and in prison may gain more criminal skills to continue reoffending when released. See the reoffending rates in the Bromley Briefings.	Social learning theory
Laws are imposed to provide equality and ensure that rules are applied equally to all people.	Marxist theory
The home environment of an offender can impact on their reoffending. A lack of employment, financial support, education and housing can influence whether or not the offender stays out of prison.	Marxist theory Labelling theory
Crimes committed by those with moral imperatives can produce boundary maintenance and show people what is acceptable in society.	Functionalism

See the case of Abu Qatada on page 27 of the textbook.

Limitations in prisons preventing social control

Provided via the Prison Reform Trust, the 'Bromley Briefings Summer 2018' (http://www.prisonreformtrust.org.uk/Portals/0/Documents/Bromley%20Briefings/Summer%202018%20factfile.pdf) states that:

Facts and figures provide a better basis than opinion for policy and practice change. Drawn largely from government sources, these facts chart the extraordinary rise in prison numbers over the last twenty years, inflation in sentencing and the social and economic consequences of overuse of custody. They reveal the state of our overcrowded prisons and the state of people in them, the impact of deep budget cuts, the pace and scale of change in the justice system and the scope for community solutions to crime.

Prisons suffer from overcrowding and a lack of resources.

Activity 4.19

Using the above online report, find the answers to the following questions, which will help you to appreciate the limitations of the prison system. Be prepared to use some of the facts in your Unit 4 exam.

1. Which country has the highest prison rate in western Europe?
2. Which country has the lowest prison rate in western Europe?
3. By how much has the prison population risen over the last 30 years?
4. How many people were sent to prison in 2017?
5. By how much has the budget for HM Prisons and Probation Service (HMPS) been reduced between 2010–2011 and 2014–2015?
6. What is the overall cost of a prison place in England and Wales?
7. What was the percentage cut for frontline operational staff between 2010 and 2017?
8. What percentage of women and men said they had received treatment for a mental health problem in the year before custody?
9. How much more likely is a self-inflicted death in prison than in the general population?
10. What percentage of adults serving less than 12 months are reconvicted within one year of release?

Example question

The following question is from the **2018 Unit 4 exam**. Using the mark scheme decide how many marks the answer would achieve.

Examine the limitations of achieving social control in prisons.
[7 marks]

0 marks: Nothing worthy of any marks.
1–3 marks: Answers provide a basic examination of the limitations in achieving social control in prisons. Answers convey meaning but lack detail. Little or no use of specialist vocabulary.
4–5 marks: Answers provide some examination of the limitations of achieving social control in prisons. Answers communicate meaning with some use of specialist vocabulary.
6–7 marks: Answers discuss in detail an examination of the limitations of achieving social control in prisons. Answers are well structured and clearly expressed. Specialist terms are used with ease and accuracy.

Read and mark the sample answer.

Sample answer

One of the limitations in achieving social control in prisons is budget cuts. By 2020 the prison service is expected to lose 40% of its funding. These funding cuts cause poor living conditions in prisons which can result in prisoners rioting (as in HMP Birmingham in 2016). A lack of money also reduces the resources to help rehabilitate the prisoners. This includes education and work being unavailable. Another limitation preventing social control in prisoners is staff shortages. A lack of staff often results in prisoners being locked down for extended periods of time. This was attributed as a cause to the riots in HMP the Mount, where in 2017 the prison riot squad was sent in twice. A lack of staff means fights cannot be stopped and a ratio of 1:30 makes social control very difficult. Finally, prisons arguably have a high percentage of prisoners with a mental illness and an inability to successfuly treat such conditions. This contributes to the growing suicide rate in prisons.

A lack of prison staff can result in prisoners spending more time in their cells.

Explore online

Watch 'Panorama – Behind Bars: Prison Undercover' on YouTube (https://www.youtube.com/watch?v=oH22T_X1Cys), a 29-minute undercover investigation, which reveals the reality of life behind bars in Britain's crisis-hit prison system. As you watch it, produce a summary of the limitations in prisons that prevent social control being achieved.

Take it further

Read 'HMP Birmingham: Government Plan to Restore Safety Unveiled' (2018, 17 September), BBC News (https://www.bbc.co.uk/news/uk-england-birmingham-45547815) and produce a summary of the government plans for HMP Birmingham as a result of the riots in 2016.

Crimes committed by those with moral imperatives

Arguably, the most famous person who committed a crime due to a moral imperative is Robin Hood, who stole from the rich to give to the poor.

Crime committed with a moral imperative	Example
Assisted suicide	Kay Gilderdale admitted a charge of aiding and abetting the suicide of her bedridden daughter, who had suffered a severe form of ME for 17 years.
Anti-vivisection crimes	Protesting against experiments on animals. For example, Luke Steele, the animal rights activist, who has been convicted of intimidation of workers at scientific laboratories.
Crimes committed by those who oppose fox hunting	There is a small number of hunt saboteurs who will break the law to try to prevent fox hunting taking place.

Despite having good motives, Robin Hood was a criminal.

Take it further

Research the case of *R v Owen* (1992) and explore the moral imperatives in the case.

ANIMAL RESEARCH IS SCIENTIFIC FRAUD

Anti-vivisectionists protesting against experiments on animals.

Other limitations preventing social control

Environment: the offender's home life following release from prison can impact on their reoffending. Aspects such as employment, financial resources, education, family support and friends can all be factors that limit social control being achieved

Access to resources and support: when these are not available, rehabilitation is limited. For instance, education skills such as literacy and numeracy are low in offenders

Limitations

Civil liberties and legal barriers: at times, these can prevent agencies such as the police achieving social control. For example, the issues around the deportation of foreign nationals who have served custodial sentences

Local and national policies: a preference to the enforcement of one policy may prevent others being successful. With restricted resources, enforcement either locally or nationally may mean a lack of control in non-priority areas

Test yourself

1. Explain how some of the criminological theories can link to the limitations in achieving social control.
2. List limitations that can prevent social control being achieved in prisons.
3. What is meant by crimes committed by those with moral imperatives? Give examples to support your answer.
4. How can civil liberties be a limitation on achieving social control?
5. How can someone's environment impact social control being achieved?

CHECKLIST – ARE YOU ABLE TO:

☐ examine the limitations of agencies in achieving social control

☐ examine how repeat offenders/recidivism affect social control being achieved

☐ examine how civil liberties and legal barriers could prevent social control being achieved

☐ examine how a lack of access to resources and support can impact on social control being achieved

☐ examine how a lack of funding in many agencies can reduce the effectiveness of social control

☐ examine how local and national policies may affect social control being achieved

☐ examine how the environment may affect social control being achieved

☐ examine how crime committed by those with moral imperatives may affect social control?

AC3.4 EVALUATE THE EFFECTIVENESS OF AGENCIES IN ACHIEVING SOCIAL CONTROL

See pages 263–271 of the textbook.

It is important to be able to evaluate the effectiveness of the following agencies in achieving social control:

- police
- CPS
- judiciary
- prison
- probation
- charities.

In other words, do the agencies achieve social control? In an exam situation an answer should include both positive and negative comments, although not necessarily in equal proportions. Examples to support your comments should also be included.

Key term

Effectiveness: the degree to which something is successful. In AC3.4 it means the degree to which the agencies achieve social control.

Example questions

The following questions have appeared in past exam papers:

Evaluate the effectiveness of the police service in achieving social control. [6 marks] **Unit 4 2018 exam paper**

Evaluate the effectiveness of social control inside prisons. [8 marks] **Unit 4 2017 exam paper**

Assess the effectiveness of one (or more) charity in achieving social control. [5 marks] **Unit 4 2018 exam paper**

The police are an effective agency in achieving social control.

Synoptic link

Think back to Unit 3, Crime scene to courtroom, and recall cases such as Colin Stagg, Stephen Lawrence and the Hillsborough investigations. For Unit 1, Changing awareness of crime, synoptic links include the issue of the police not recording crimes and the past attitude of the police in domestic abuse crimes and honour crimes.

Exam tip

Remember to include both positive and negative points when considering the effectiveness of the agencies in achieving social control.

Effectiveness of the police

Police achieving social control		
Positives	**Negatives**	**Examples**
Work with the community keeping law and order.	Police closing cases without identifying a suspect. For instance, in 2017 almost half of all cases were closed without a suspect being identified.	The case of Stephen Lawrence resulted in the Macpherson Report, which labelled the police 'institutionally racist'.
Expertise with specialist operations such as anti-terrorism, firearms and covert operations and intelligence.	Rise in crime rates as identified by the Office for National Statistics. In July 2017 the Home Office reported that crime had risen by 10%.	The police were condemned by the judge in the Colin Stagg case. He called the undercover operation 'deceptive conduct of the grossest kind'.
Willingness to change to be more effective, especially with changing crimes such as technological crimes.	Failure by the police to record crimes reported to them. This can be up to a fifth of all crime, including serious offences such as sexual offences, domestic abuse and rape.	Other recent cases where the police have been criticised include 'The Puppy Farm Murder' and the disorder in Cromer in 2017.
The police are held to account, for instance by Police and Crime Commissioners.		

Example question

In the **Unit 4 2018 exam paper** the following question appeared:

Evaluate the effectiveness of the police service in achieving social control. [6 marks]

Use the mark scheme below to decide the mark for the answer that follows.

0 marks: Nothing worthy of any marks.

1–2 marks: Answers describe in basic detail the effectiveness of the police service in achieving social control. Little or no evaluation. Answers convey some meaning but lack detail and may be more of a list. Little or no use of specialist vocabulary.

3–4 marks: Answers evaluate in some detail the effectiveness of the police service in achieving social control. Answers communicate meaning with some use of specialist vocabulary.

5–6 marks: Answers evaluate in detail the effectiveness of the police service in achieving social control. Answers are well structured and clearly expressed. Specialist terms are used with ease and accuracy.

Past exam papers are a great source of revision material.

Sample answer

The police service can be effective in achieving social control as they act as a deterrence to prevent crime being committed. Potential criminals see that they will be arrested, charged and placed before the courts but prefer to have their freedom. The police service is national and hence have a wide presence. However, a lack of funding may mean they are not as effective as they could be. There are insufficient officers on the streets and crimes cannot always be detected. The police are restricted by only being able to investigate crime if offences are reported to them. The dark figure of crime can mean no detection or investigation.

Explore online

Read 'Is Rise in Violent Crime Due to Cuts to Neighbourhood Policing?' by Jamie Grierson (2018, 9 April), the *Guardian* (https://www.theguardian.com/uk-news/2018/apr/09/rise-in-violent-not-due-to-police-cuts-alone-figures-show), about a rise in violent crime due to cuts to neighbourhood policing, then summarise the main points in 100 words.

The effectiveness of the Crown Prosecution Service and judiciary in achieving social control

Agency	Positive	Negative	Examples
CPS	Independent agency. Use of the full codes test to decide on prosecution brings a uniform and fair approach. Promotes the rights of victims and witnesses.	Centralised and bureaucratic. Too close to the police. Failed rape cases where there was a failure to disclose documents.	Glidewell Report 1998. Narey Report. Case of Abu Hamza. Case of Damilola Taylor. Lord Janner's prosecution
Judiciary	An authority figure ensuring trials are fair and human rights compliant. An experienced and highly qualified lawyer. Uses a system of precedent to ensure consistency and fairness.	Increasing number of appeals for unduly lenient sentences. Are criticised as being out of touch with society and unrepresentative of it.	Judge lets off thief and commends his enterprise. Judge lets former drug dealer off unpaid work because of transport issues. Judge lets off sex abuser then blames victim.

The Crown Prosecution Service is a government-funded agency.

For more about 'Judge lets off thief and commends his enterprise' see page 267 of the textbook.

Take it further »»»

Read 'Urgent Review of all Rape Cases as Digital Evidence is Withheld' by Owen Bowcott (2018, 27 January), the *Guardian* (https://www.theguardian.com/society/2018/jan/26/urgent-review-of-all-cases-as-digital-evidence-is-withheld) and produce a short paragraph for use in an exam situation about the CPS failing to disclose evidence in rape cases.

The judiciary is an experienced and highly qualified body imposing social control in the courts.

The effectiveness of prisons in achieving social control

Example question

Evaluate the effectiveness of social control inside prisons.
[8 marks] **Unit 4 2017 exam paper**

Sample answer

Positive effects:

· Protection of society.
· Prevention of crime.
· Rehabilitation of offenders.
· Reparation to society.
· Education/training of offenders.

The effectiveness of prisons in achieving social control is rarely out of the news.

Negative effects:

· Criminal offences are committed, e.g. while in prison, which suggests that social control might not be achieved.
· Disturbances in prisons, e.g. HMP Birmingham riots in 2016 or riot at HMP Oakwood in 2014.
· Significant rise in prison disturbances and callouts of the National Tactical Response group (prison's anti-riot squad).
· Serious attacks within prison are at a record high.
· Attacks on prison officers.
· Use of prohibited drugs such as spice and their availability within prisons.
· Low literacy and numeracy ages of prisoners.
· Mental health issues of prisoners.
· Increase in suicide rates in prison.

Activity 4.20

Find on the internet 'Conditions at HMP Nottingham "May Have Caused Suicides"', (2018, 16 May), BBC News (http://www. bbc.co.uk/news/uk-england-nottinghamshire-44126087).

It is an article following an inspection of HMP Nottingham. It starts by suggesting that *'Inmates may have taken their own lives at Nottingham Prison because they could no longer face life at the "drug-ridden jail".'*

Read the article and produce a summary of the main points.

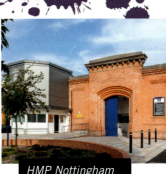

HMP Nottingham has been described as a dangerous jail.

Effectiveness of the probation service in achieving social control

PROBATION

AC3.4 includes the effectiveness of probation in achieving social control.

One of the biggest criticisms of the probation service is its attempt at part privatisation. This resulted in the government agency working in partnership with 21 community rehabilitation companies (CRCs). The aim was for the National Probation Service to monitor offenders who were designated as being at high risk to the public. The CRC's role was to monitor mid- and low-risk offenders. However, the joint report in 2017 by the Inspectorate of Probation and the Inspectorate of Prisons was very critical of the changes.

See details of the criticisms on page 269 of the textbook.

As a result of the problems within the system it was announced in 2018 that the government would terminate the contracts with the CRCs in 2020, two years earlier than agreed.

Effectiveness of charities in achieving social control

It is important that you include charities or pressure groups in many of the ACs, including AC3.4. You can select any charities as long as they are focused around the Criminal Justice System and attempt to work towards social control. The key feature is to ensure you can comment of their effectiveness regarding social control. It would therefore be helpful to include examples such as campaigns and their achievements. Examples of charities could include:

- Prison Reform Trust
- Catch 22
- Prince's Trust
- Howard League for Penal Reform
- Clinks
- Criminal Justice Alliance.

Explore online

Read 'Conner Marshall: Killer's Probation Monitoring "Shambolic"' (2017, 25 October), BBC News (https://www.bbc.co.uk/news/uk-wales-south-east-wales-41748185) and make notes of the murder of 18-year-old Connor Marshall by David Braddon, who was subject to a probation order at the time of the killing.

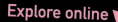

Explore online

To appreciate the importance of charities in the criminal justice system read 'The UK's Criminal Justice System Would Fall Apart Without Charities' by Nathan Dick (2017, 12 July), the *Guardian* (https://www.theguardian.com/voluntary-sector-network/2017/jul/12/criminal-justice-charities-prison-probation).

The table below summarises the effectiveness of three main charities in the criminal justice system.

Charity	Positives	Negatives
Prison Reform Trust PRISON REFORM TRUST	Work towards a humane and effective penal system. 'Care not Custody' campaign prompted the government to develop mental health services within police stations and courts for vulnerable suspects. Work helped secure £50 million investment from the government for the above schemes. There is now a Care not Custody coalition to continue to promote the issue of mental health within prisons.	Does not receive government funding. Survives by voluntary donations. There are many charities working in the field of social control that compete with each other.
Prince's Trust Prince's Trust YOUTH CAN DO IT	Focuses on young people aged 11–30, empowering them to obtain jobs, education and training. Includes young people who have been in trouble with the law. Have helped more than 950,000 young people since 1976. Principal fundraising event, Invest in Futures, has raised over £22 million to invest in the lives of young people since 2005. One programme helps to reduce offending, the Team Programme, is a 12-week personal development programme for 16 to 25-year-olds to develop their confidence, motivation and skills through teamwork in the community. More than 210,000 young people across the country have participated in The Trust's 12-week Team programme since its launch in 1990.	There are many charities working in the field of social control that compete with each other.

(Continued)

Charity	Positives	Negatives
Howard League for Penal Reform	The country's oldest penal reform charity, established in 1866.	Does not receive government funding.
	Aims for less crime, safer communities and fewer people in prison.	Survives by voluntary donations.
	The Books for Prisoners campaign argued against restrictions on prisoners receiving books from friends and family. The campaign was successful and the charity won an award in 2015 in recognition of its work.	There are many charities working in the field of social control that compete with each other.
	In 2003 the charity took the government to court and argued that the Children Act 1989 must also apply to children in custody. It won the case and secured welfare support for children in and out of custody.	

Take it further

Read about the action taken by the charity in the area of mental health and prisons on the Prison Reform Trust website, 'PRT Comment: HMP Wakefield' (http://www.prisonreformtrust.org.uk/PressPolicy/News/Mentalhealth).

Read some of the individual success stories brought about by the Prince's Trust on its website, 'You Can Do It' (https://www.princes-trust.org.uk/about-the-trust/success-stories).

Read 'Our Success' on the Howard League for Penal Reform website (https://howardleague.org/what-you-can-do/our-success/) and make a note of more success stories from the charity.

Test yourself

1. Name all the agencies you could be asked to evaluate the effectiveness of as regards achieving social control.
2. Explain how the case of Stephen Lawrence could impact on the effectiveness of the police in achieving social control.
3. Explain the role of Police and Crime Commissioners.
4. What is meant by the phrase 'the CPS is an independent agency'?
5. Do you think the judiciary are representative of society?
6. In your opinion, what is the main limitation of the prison service in achieving social control?
7. Explain the involvement of community rehabilitation companies in achieving social control.
8. What part do charities and pressure groups play in achieving social control?

DEBATE

Activity 4.21

Class debate

Research the suggestion that prison sentences under six months should be abolished as they are ineffective at achieving social control.

The class should then be divided into two – one side in favour of the proposal and one against – and hold a debate.

CHECKLIST – ARE YOU ABLE TO:

☐ evaluate the effectiveness of the following agencies in achievement social control:
- policing
- CPS
- judiciary
- prison
- probation
- charities

☐ ensure that you can give a balanced view including examples to support your comments?

SKILLS GUIDANCE

WHY HAVE THIS SECTION?

One of the main reasons students do not achieve the marks they hoped to achieve is because they do not understand what the question is asking. Often a question does not just ask for information on a topic but rather it requires information provided in a particular way. For instance, it may require a discussion of a topic or a break-down of the main points. Frequently, a question needs the positive and negative aspects of a topic rather than general points in an answer. It is therefore important that you appreciate how the information must be provided.

The importance of command words

Each AC in every unit has a command word at the start of the heading. The following table has examples from each unit.

Unit 1	Unit 2	Unit 3	Unit 4
AC1.1 **Analyse** different types of crime	AC1.1 **Compare** criminal behaviour and deviance	AC1.4 **Examine** the rights of individuals in criminal investigations	AC3.3 **Examine** the limitations of agencies in achieving social control
AC1.4 **Describe** media representation of crime	AC3.2 **Evaluate** the effectiveness of criminological theories to explain causes of criminality	AC2.1 **Explain** the requirements of the Crown Prosecution Service (CPS) for prosecuting suspects	AC3.4 **Evaluate** the effectiveness of agencies in achieving social control
AC3.3 **Justify** a campaign for change	AC4.1 **Assess** the use of criminological theories in informing policy development	AC2.5 **Discuss** the use of laypeople in criminal cases	AC3.1 **Explain** the role of agencies in social control

Command verbs

The following are definitions to help your understanding of command verbs:

- **Analyse**: examine in detail, break into component parts, examine relationships.
- **Assess**: make a judgement about the quality or value of something.
- **Compare**: explain similarities and differences.
- **Define**: state the meaning of a term.
- **Describe**: paint a picture in words, provide information with detail. Using this analogy, you would expect there to be some detail in the answer.
- **Design**: prepare materials such as a plan or drawing to show the look and function of something.
- **Draw conclusions**: decide on particular facts or principles from information given.
- **Evaluate**: make judgements about the quality or importance of something against criteria, usually based on analysis and data. Often includes the strengths and weaknesses of the topic.
- **Examine**: look at something carefully and in detail in order to discover something about the topic.
- **Explain**: give reasons.
- **Identify**: recognise, distinguish and establish what something is.
- **Illustrate**: exemplify, describe with reference to examples.
- **Justify**: persuade someone of the validity of an argument; validate a proposal.
- **Outline**: give a sketch of the situation, give an overall impression. A good outline becomes a description.
- **Plan**: to decide on and make arrangements for something in advance.
- **State**: make an assertion.
- **Understand**: know the meaning of something or know why or how something happens or works.

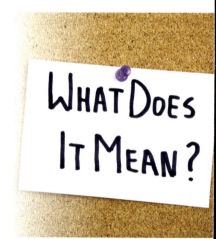

In answers, the examiner or moderator will differentiate the mark awarded to an answer by looking for the following:

- **Accuracy**: is what being claimed as fact actually correct?
- **Breadth/range**: is there an expectation of breadth rather than depth, i.e. you should have superficial knowledge of a lot of facts rather than in-depth knowledge of a few.
- **Clarity**: often related to communication skills, but you can anticipate that someone who really knows something knows how to organise what they are saying and doesn't mix fact with information that is incorrect or irrelevant. People who waffle tend to be less certain of their knowledge than those who can be succinct and to the point.

- **Depth/detail**: have you given sufficient detail to confirm that you really do know something?
- **Relevance/application**: do the facts have to be relevant to the situation? Is it simply pure theory or do you want to show knowledge through the discarding of what is considered irrelevant?
- **Justification**: would someone be persuaded by your argument and reasoning?
- **Substantiation**: have you drawn on evidence to support any conclusions made?
- **Validity**: is the reasoning valid? Is it accurate? Is it based on the context of the situation? Is it based on theory?

Main command words

Now let us consider some of the main command words used in the specifications.

Analyse

Analyse means to examine in detail, break into component parts or examine relationships. The following ACs feature this command word:

Unit 1	Unit 2
AC1.1 Analyse different types of crime	AC3.1 Analyse situations of criminality

This is how 'analyse' works for Unit 2 AC3.1.

Analyse situations of criminality. You must break-down into different parts the reasoning for crime occurring. The information in the question should give you clues about something that may be responsible for the criminality. This would be different for each of the three theories of criminality, i.e. biological, individualistic or sociological. By the time you are asked to analyse situations of criminality in an exam you already will have described one theory. Breaking down that theory and matching it to the appropriate part of the exam scenario you will be analysing.

For example, question 1 on the **Unit 2 2017 exam paper** had the following:

Paul, an unemployed local man, was convicted of murder. He was convicted after getting into a fight with Ian over an allegation of theft of money. Paul also has numerous previous convictions for drug dealing and theft. He has been in care since the age of seven, after his parents were given long custodial sentences. Ian's father, a local barrister, has started a campaign to bring back capital punishment for crimes of murder. His campaign has attracted the attention of local media and politicians.

185

Break-down the information in the scenario into possible links to criminality and you get the following:

- unemployed local man
- in care since the age of seven
- his parents were given long custodial sentences.

Depending on the theory you have already described in the exam, you must break-down that theory into aspects that are relevant to any of the above points. For example, if you have described the social learning theory you may break it down into the following points:

- unemployed local man – has a low income and may have learned that the rewards from crime are positive.
- in care since the age of seven – may have learned from those around him; peer group may be role models.
- his parents were given long custodial sentences – links to earning criminality from his parents; family are main role models.

The above bullet list shows a break-down of information or an analysis of it.

Exam tip ✔

Analyse is a term that is very likely to appear an exam question. It will be linked to a scenario or factual information and will require you to break it down into parts to consider.

Evaluate

Evaluate means to make judgements against criteria, usually based on analysis and data. The following ACs feature this command word.

Unit 1	Unit 2	Unit 3	Unit 4
AC1.6 Evaluate methods of collecting statistics about crime AC2.2 Evaluate the effectiveness of media used in campaigns for change	AC3.2 Evaluate the effectiveness of criminological theories to explain causes of criminality	AC1.1 Evaluate the effectiveness of the roles of personnel involved in criminal investigations	AC3.4 Evaluate the effectiveness of agencies in achieving social control

EVALUATION

Evaluation appears in every unit.

Also see page 77 AC3.2 Evaluate the effectiveness of criminological theories to explain causes of criminality for more detail on evaluation.

This is how it works for Unit 4 AC3.4:

Evaluate the effectiveness of agencies in achieving social control. You must make a judgement about different agencies to decide whether or not they achieve social control. For example, using the agency of the police, on the following page is a table with information broken down into positives and negatives, or strengths and weaknesses, linked to social control. This can also be found on page 176. Note that there are examples and statistics to help make a judgement.

Police achieving social control		
Positives	**Negatives**	**Examples**
• Work with the community in keeping law and order. • Expertise with the socialist operations such as anti-terrorism, firearms and covert operations and intelligence. • Willingness to change to be more effective especially with changing crimes such as technological crimes. • The police are held to account for instance by Police and Crime Commissioners.	• Closing cases without identifying a suspect. For instance, in 2017 almost half of all cases were closed without a suspect being identified. • Rise in crime rates as identified by the Office for National Statistics. In July 2017 the Home Office reported that crime had risen by 10%. • Failure by the police to record crimes reported to them. This can be up to a fifth of all crime including serious offences which include sexual offences, domestic abuse and rape.	• The case of Stephen Lawrence resulted in the Macpherson Report which labelled the police 'institutionally racist'. • The police were condemned by the judge in the Colin Stagg case. He called the undercover operation 'deceptive conduct of the grossest kind'. • Other recent cases where the police have been criticised include 'the Puppy Farm Murder' and the disorder in Cromer in 2017.

Compare

Compare means to explain similarities and differences. The following ACs feature this command word.

Unit 1	Unit 2
AC2.1 Compare campaigns for change	AC1.1 Compare criminal behaviour and deviance

It is important to look at both similarities and differences when you compare.

This is how it works for Unit 2 AC1.1:

Compare criminal behaviour and deviance. Below is a table which can also be found on page 47. It shows similarities and differences for the terms crime and deviance.

Criminal behaviour only	Deviance only	Criminal behaviour and deviance
Acts that break the rules, deemed to be illegal by the law-making powers of a society. For example, murder or assault. Such acts result in punishment by the police (such as a caution) or by a court (such as a fine or imprisonment).	Acts that are against social norms. For example, shouting in a library or cross-dressing. Such acts result in sanctions from others in society such as name calling or ignoring the deviant person.	Some crimes can be against social norms such as theft or fraud but crimes such as speeding and illegal downloading of music are sometimes so commonplace that they are not deemed to be considered deviant.

Example question

Compare criminality and deviance with reference to relevant examples. [5 marks] **Unit 2 2017 exam paper**

To compare something, it is appropriate to include relevant terminology to show comparisons are taking place. For example:

- in comparison
- whereas
- in contrast
- but

- similarly
- likewise
- to the contrary.

To assess means you must make a judgement as to the value of something.

ASSESSMENT

Assess

Assess means to make a judgement about the quality or value of something. The following ACs feature this command word.

Unit 2	Unit 3	Unit 4
AC4.1 Assess the use of criminological theories in informing policy development	AC1.2 Assess the usefulness of investigative techniques in criminal investigations AC2.4 Assess key influences affecting the outcomes of criminal cases	AC2.3 Assess how forms of punishment meet the aims of punishment

This is how it works for Unit 4 AC2.3:

> Assess how forms of punishment meet the aims of punishment. You must make a judgement about whether or not the types of punishment (e.g. custodial sentences, community sentences, financial penalties or discharges) achieve the identified aims of punishments (e.g. retribution, rehabilitation, reparation, etc.). To assess you need information to make a judgement. Such information would need to be factual and could contain data and statistics or examples to support your judgement.

The following, from 'Bromley Briefings' Summer 2018 by the Prison Reform Trust, focuses on information to help assess whether or not prison achieves any aims of punishment. It can also be found at page 153.

England and Wales has the highest imprisonment rate in Western Europe.

The prison population has risen by 77% in the last 30 years.

65,000 people were sent to prison to serve a sentence in 2017.

Short prison sentences are less effective than community sentences at reducing reoffending.

People serving mandatory life sentences are spending more of their sentence in prison. On average they spend 17 years in custody, up from 13 years in 2001.

Many of our prisons are overcrowded – and have been for a long time. Overcrowding affects whether activities, staff and other resources are available to reduce risk of reoffending, as well as distance from families and other support networks.

Many are released from prison, only to return there shortly after.

The number of people recalled back to custody has increased, particularly among women. 8,825 people serving a sentence of less than 12 months were recalled to prison in the year to December 2017.

Prison has a poor record for reducing reoffending – nearly half of adults (48%) are reconvicted within one year of release. For those serving sentences of less than 12 months this increases to 64%.

It could be argued that, as so many people are sent to prison, retribution is achieved. While offenders are in prison public protection also is achieved. However, given the reoffending rates, rehabilitation does not appear to be successful.

GLOSSARY OF KEY TERMS

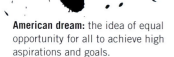

American dream: the idea of equal opportunity for all to achieve high aspirations and goals.

Analyse: examine in detail, break into component parts, examine relationships.

Anomie: loss of shared principles or norms.

Assess: to make a judgement about the quality or value of something.

Biological: relating to processes or activities concerned with living things. For our purposes it relates to the body, both inside and outside, as reasons for committing crimes.

Bourgeoisie: the middle and upper classes who own the means of production in industry.

Capital punishment: also known as the death penalty, is the legally authorised killing of someone as punishment for a crime.

Compare: explain similarities and differences.

Crime: breaches of rules set as criminal by a society.

Criminogenic: causing or likely to cause criminal behaviour.

Culture: the ideas, customs and social behaviour of a particular people or society.

Culture-bound crime: tends to belong to a particular culture. Examples may include honour killing, witchcraft and female genital mutilation.

Demographics: information about a particular population.

Deviance: acts against social norms.

Domestic abuse: an incident or pattern of incidents of controlling, coercive, threatening, degrading and violent behaviour, including sexual violence, in the majority of cases by a partner or ex-partner, but could also be by a family member or carer.

Ecological validity: the extent to which the findings of a research study are able to be generalised to real-life settings.

Effectiveness: the degree to which something is successful. In AC3.4 it means the degree to which the agencies achieve social control.

Environment: the surroundings in which a person lives.

Eugenics: the science of improving a population by controlled breeding, to increase the occurrence of desirable heritable characteristics.

Evaluate: to what extent do you agree with the theory? Make a judgement about the quality or importance of a theory by providing strengths and weaknesses of how well the theory supports the reason for criminality. Ideally, come to a conclusion and justify how you have made your choice.

Examine: inspect, scrutinise or observe.

Genetic: relating to genes or heredity.

Hate crimes: targeted at a person because of hostility or prejudice towards the person's disability, race or ethnicity, religion or belief, sexual orientation or transgender identity.

Impact: the effect or consequence of something. In this instance, what effect the media representation of crime has on the public.

Individualistic: relating to an individual rather than society as a whole.

Inform: to give knowledge or have an impact/effect.

Judicial: belonging or related to a judge.

Justify: explain with good reasons what you have done and why you have chosen to do it.

Limitations: something that controls or reduces something.

Miscarriage of justice: a criminal case where the defendant has been convicted for a crime which he/she did not commit. It is the conviction of an innocent person.

Model: a system or a procedure used as an example to follow.

Moral crimes: crimes against morality, often considered to be victimless crimes because there is no specific victim.

Neurochemicals: chemicals which can transfer signals that can regulate thoughts and emotions.

Physiology: the functions of living organisms, in our case human beings and their parts, and, in particular, the way in which they function.

Politics: the activities linked to the governance of a country.

Precedent: a decision in a legal case that must be followed in similar future cases.

Proletariat: the lower social class, who must provide their labour to the upper classes for a wage.

Public perception: the perceived level of crime in a particular place, or the perceived severity of crimes. It is the opinion or belief held by the public. Generally, it is a collective opinion.

Relative deprivation: how someone feels in relation to others or compared with their own expectations.

Slogan: a short and memorable phrase often used for the purpose of advertising.

Social construction: something based on the collective views developed and maintained within a society or social group.

Tag line: a catchy or short, snappy statement that usually promotes action or persuades the audience to do something or think a particular way.

Technological crimes: committed using a computer and the internet or other electronic technologies.

Validity: does it have authority, weight, strength or soundness? In other words, it is accurate? For example, ask if a verdict from a criminal case is a valid decision or not?

White-collar crimes: non-violent crimes traditionally committed in commercial situations for financial gain. White-collar crime is largely committed by a business person wearing a suit and tie.

INDEX